The *Bakke* Case and the Affirmative Action Debate

Debating Supreme Court Decisions

Stephanie Sammartino McPherson

Enslow Publishers, Inc.

40 Industrial Road	PO Box 38
Box 398	Aldershot
Berkeley Heights, NJ 07922	Hants GU12 6BP
USA	UK

http://www.enslow.com

To Dick

Library of Congress Cataloging-in-Publication Data

McPherson, Stephanie Sammartino.
    The Bakke case and the affirmative action debate : debating Supreme Court
decisions / Stephanie Sammartino McPherson.
        p. cm. — (Debating Supreme Court decisions)
    Includes bibliographical references and index.
    ISBN 0-7660-2526-8
    1. Bakke, Allan Paul—Trials, litigation, etc.—Juvenile literature. 2. University
of California (System). Regents—Trials, litigation, etc.—Juvenile literature.
3. Discrimination in medical education—Law and legislation—United States—Juvenile
literature. 4. Affirmative action programs in education—Law and legislation—United
States—Juvenile literature. 5. Medical colleges—California—Admission—Juvenile
literature. I. Title. II. Series.
    KF228.B34M47 2005
    344.73'0798—dc22

                                                    2005004189

Printed in the United States of America

10 9 8 7 6 5 4 3 2 1

To Our Readers: We have done our best to make sure that all Internet Addresses in this
book were active and appropriate when we went to press. However, the author and publisher
have no control over and assume no liability for the material available on those Internet sites
or on other Web sites they may link to. Any comments or suggestions can be sent by e-mail
to comments@enslow.com or to the address on the back cover.

Illustration Credits: AP/Wide World, pp. 7, 53, 66, 82, 95; Hemera Image
Express, p. 2; Library of Congress, pp. 18, 21, 31; National Archives and Records
Administration, p. 41.

Cover Illustrations: Background, Artville; photograph, AP/Wide World.

Contents

Acknowledgments

Special thanks to Sam Hunter, M.D., for his thorough reading and thought-provoking comments on the manuscript, and to W. Avon Drake, Ph.D., for recommending sources and for his own excellent book, *Affirmative Action and the Stalled Quest for Black Power*. Thanks also to Janis Sammartino and to Joseph Sammartino Gardner for reading the manuscript, and to my husband, Richard McPherson, whose encouragement keeps me going.

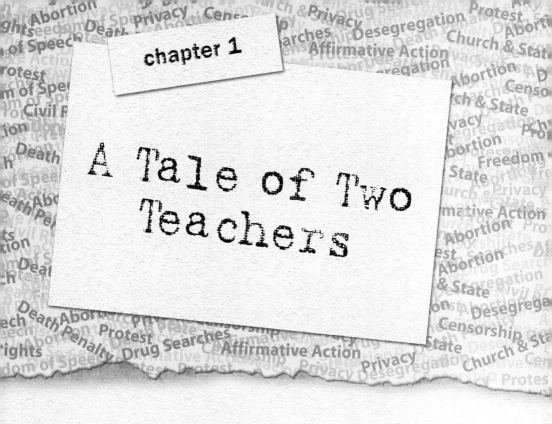

chapter 1

A Tale of Two Teachers

Debra Williams and Sharon Taxman had a great deal in common. Both women were outstanding business teachers. Both taught at Piscataway High School in New Jersey. In fact, both had been hired on the very same day. For nine years it had not mattered that Williams was African American and Taxman was white. Then, in 1989, something happened to change all that.

Fewer students were enrolling in business classes at the high school. That meant that the business department had too many teachers. In order to cut costs, the school board decided to lay off one of those teachers. But who would that be? Usually in a situation like this, the person who had been hired most recently would be the one to leave. That placed Williams and Taxman in a tie.

The school board might have drawn lots to see which teacher would keep her job. Instead, they came up with a different plan. Debra Williams would stay at the school because she was African American. Without Williams, the entire business department would be composed of white teachers. The board felt it was important to keep a racially diverse faculty. "There was an awareness that it is desirable not just for black kids to see black teachers but for white kids to see black teachers," Theodore Kruse, the president of the school board, said later.[1] Sharon Taxman was told that she was a fine teacher but that the board had relied on its "commitment to affirmative action" in making its decision.[2]

Fourteen years earlier, the school board had adopted its affirmative action policy to encourage African Americans and other minorities to apply for jobs.[3] According to the plan, the most qualified candidate would be hired regardless of his or her ethnic background. When two or more teachers appeared equally suited for a job, the board would recommend that the minority candidate be hired.

As might be expected, Sharon Taxman was shocked and disappointed by the decision. She had worked hard at her job and felt she had just as much right to stay in her classroom as Debra

Sharon Taxman and Debra Williams were high school business teachers hired on the same day. When one teacher had to be laid off, the school district chose to keep Williams because she is African American.

Williams did. But the board refused to change its ruling. After weighing her options carefully, Taxman filed a complaint with the Equal Employment Opportunities Commission (EEOC). She felt her civil rights had been violated.

Strong Reactions

Taxman's situation prompted strong reaction on both sides. Some people felt that racial diversity was such an important goal that it outweighed other factors. Yes, it was unfortunate that Taxman lost her job, they said, but the school board had the right to give preference to African Americans.

Many others sympathized with Taxman and felt she had been treated unfairly. They thought that race should play no role in the hiring or firing process.

The EEOC agreed that Taxman had a strong case—so strong, in fact, that the government filed a lawsuit against the Piscataway Board of Education.[4] Was Taxman fired illegally? By the time that question was answered, another teacher had left the business department, and Taxman had been hired back. But Taxman had lost over $144,000 in back salary and in medical benefits. She still had a big stake in the outcome of the case.[5]

On September 9, 1993, more than two years after Taxman's dismissal, the district court decided against the school board. The Civil Rights Act of 1964 forbids firing someone on the basis of race, the court declared. What happened to Taxman was a clear case of discrimination. She had lost her job simply because she was white.

Most members of the school board still believed that they had acted within the bounds of the law. Surely they had a right to do what was best for the school. And they firmly believed it was in the school's best interest to have at least one African American in the business department. Her very presence promoted racial tolerance and served as an inspiration to all students. By a 6–2 vote, the board of education decided to appeal the decision.

"This Is My Case!"

Through no fault of their own, Taxman and Williams found themselves on opposite sides of a continuing lawsuit. Taxman had lost back pay, but Williams thought she had lost something too. She was a highly qualified teacher. Because of the court case, many people overlooked her education and experience. They saw her as someone who kept her position *solely* because she was African American.[6]

Although her job was secure, Williams cared passionately about the outcome. She went to hear the lawyers hammer out the issues at the 3rd Circuit Court of Appeals in Philadelphia. By this time, the case had sparked attention from all over the country. The courtroom was so jammed that there were not enough seats. Williams was asked to leave. "This is my case!" she protested. "I belong in this courtroom!"[7]

A Lightning Rod

Although the government had initially backed Sharon Taxman and the school system, the Clinton administration withdrew support. It considered affirmative action too important to oppose. The court did not agree. It sided with Taxman a second time. The Piscataway school district was ordered to pay $144,000 to Taxman to compensate for her lost pay and for aggravation. Once again, the Piscataway Board of Education balked at the decision. The members still felt that the government had no business interfering with their efforts to achieve racial diversity. There was only one recourse left. The board members decided to appeal to the United States Supreme Court.

It was a stressful time for both teachers. Williams's husband, Alvin, thought there were two victims in the case. "You and Sharon Taxman have both been judged by the color of your skin," he told his wife. "This situation violates the principle that civil rights stands on. The board did both of you wrong. . . . You should be teamed up together."[8]

But although Williams and Taxman taught in adjacent classrooms, they barely spoke to each other. Meanwhile, the approaching Supreme Court showdown was attracting national attention. David B. Rubin, the school board's lawyer, called the case "the lightning rod in a stormy national debate over affirmative action."[9]

Many observers found it likely that the Court would uphold the rulings in favor of Taxman. Those who felt that affirmative action had gone too far and was hurting nonminorities looked forward to this decision.

On the other hand, supporters of affirmative

action did not feel that the Taxman case was right for the Supreme Court. Sharon Taxman's predicament was a very unusual one. In most cases involving affirmative action, race is one of many factors. In *Taxman* v. *Piscataway Board of Education*, race was the *only* factor. But the Court might issue statements that went well beyond Taxman's unique situation. Schools and businesses all over the country might be affected.[10]

Could the case be stopped from going to the Supreme Court? Several civil rights groups began to investigate the possibility. As far as they were concerned, the whole future of affirmative action was at stake.

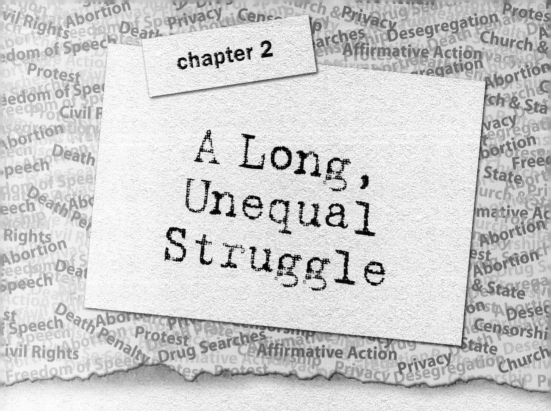

chapter 2

A Long, Unequal Struggle

Just thirty years earlier, a case such as *Taxman* v. *Piscataway Board of Education* would have been unthinkable. White citizens like Sharon Taxman did not suffer racial discrimination; African-American citizens did. Slavery had ended in the United States with the passage of the Thirteenth Amendment in 1865. But freedom did not bring African Americans the equality that should have been theirs. Neither did the Fourteenth Amendment, which made them citizens, or the Fifteenth Amendment, which gave African-American men the right to vote.

Many white people opposed the new legal status. Some of them worked actively against the strides black citizens made in the brief period after the Civil War known as the Reconstruction. Organizations such as the Knights of the White Camellia and the Ku Klux Klan used terrorism to prevent African Americans from interacting with whites and from voting.

In the South, state legislators introduced measures, such as literacy tests, to keep African Americans from voting. "Grandfather clauses" allowed whites—even those who could not read— to get out of the literacy test. Grandfather clauses were provisions in the laws of several Southern states that allowed people to vote if they were the descendants of men who voted before 1867. Of course, that was no help to blacks whose grandfathers had been slaves. The poll tax was another major obstacle that blacks had to face. Most African-American families lived on less than $100 a year. They could not afford a single dollar for the poll tax.[1]

Even the Supreme Court declined to protect the rights of African Americans. In the 1880s, the Court declared that it was up to the states to guarantee the rights of black citizens. Instead, the Southern states continued to do the opposite. A series of regulations, known as Jim Crow laws, were passed in the 1890s. These enforced a rigid separation between blacks and whites in all public areas, including buses, trains, schools, and restaurants.

Frederick Douglass, the famous African American who worked so hard to end slavery, was outraged. Speaking at the Chicago World's Fair in 1893, he urged Americans to uphold the Constitution for all people. "We Negroes love our country. We fought for it. We ask only that we be treated as well as those who fought against it."[2]

Plessy v. *Ferguson*

Just one year before Douglass's stirring words, some prominent African-American leaders in Louisiana decided to challenge a law that forced blacks to travel in separate railway cars. A thirty-year-old shoemaker named Homer Plessy agreed to help. On June 7, 1892, Plessy boarded a train in New Orleans that was bound for Covington, Louisiana. Although he was mostly white, Plessy had one African-American great-grandparent and so was considered black by state law. Seating himself in a car marked "Whites Only," Plessy ignored a demand from the conductor to leave. Soon afterward, the train ground to a standstill. A detective clambered on board to arrest Plessy.

The court case that ensued eventually made its way to the Supreme Court. Plessy's lawyers argued that the Separate Car Law marked "the colored race with a badge of inferiority."[3] The Supreme Court disagreed. In *Plessy* v. *Ferguson*, a ruling that has become infamous, the Court upheld

Louisiana's right to make laws separating blacks and whites.

The only dissenting vote came from Justice John Marshall Harlan, who wrote:

> Our Constitution is color-blind, and neither knows nor tolerates classes among citizens. In respect of civil rights, all citizens are equal before the law. . . . I am of the opinion that the statute of Louisiana is inconsistent with the personal liberty of citizens, white and black, in that State, and hostile to both the spirit and letter of the Constitution of the United States. If laws of like character should be enacted in several States of the Union, the effect would be in the highest degree mischievous.[4]

Separate but Equal

The *Plessy* v. *Ferguson* decision was used to support the doctrine of "separate but equal." It enabled the passage of still more Jim Crow laws that separated the races. In many places, African Americans were not allowed to use the same restrooms or water fountains as white people. They were buried in separate cemeteries. Feelings ran so strong that President Theodore Roosevelt caused an uproar in 1901 simply by dining with African-American educator Booker T. Washington in the White House.

Despite the "separate but equal " doctrine, the schools that African-American children were required to attend in the South did not meet the same standards as the schools that white children enjoyed. In the late 1930s, author Gunnar Myrdal, who visited an African-American school in Georgia, was distressed to find children from six to seventeen sharing the same classroom. Although this was not uncommon in rural areas, the teacher's time was spread out too thinly. Students did not get all the attention they needed. Because she had not been to college, the teacher was not well qualified to help them. To Myrdal's further dismay, none of the children could name the president of the United States.[5] In many areas of the South, local governments provided no high school education at all for African-American students. Before the Civil War, it had been illegal to teach black children to read and write. By 1940, more than 10 percent of black citizens in the United States were still illiterate.[6]

The Winds of Change

The end of World War II brought great changes to the United States and renewed hope for African Americans. They had worked hard to help win the war. Although military units were segregated, there were times when black soldiers and white soldiers fought side by side. General Buck Lanham had praised the African-American troops who fought in the Battle of the Bulge. "I have never seen any soldiers who have performed better in combat than you," he told them.[7] At home, black citizens had held down important jobs in the war industries. The war had been waged in the name of freedom and democracy. Many African Americans felt it was time to fulfill their own dreams. They began applying to colleges and graduate schools in record numbers.[8]

Sweatt v. Painter

In 1946, a year after the war ended, Heman Sweatt, a thirty-three-year-old African-American mail carrier, applied to law school at the University of Texas. Despite meeting the entrance requirements, he was refused admittance. No black law schools existed in Texas. If Sweatt wanted to become a lawyer, he would have to go north. Instead, backed by the National Association for the Advancement of Colored People (NAACP), he filed a lawsuit.

The district court saw the soundness of Sweatt's reasoning. The young man had as much right to a legal education in his home state as anyone else. But the judge did not order the school to admit Sweatt. He gave the state a deadline of six months to develop a law program for African-American students that was "substantially equivalent" to the one offered for white students at the University of Texas.[9]

State officials got right to work. In record time the Texas State University for Negroes opened in

Heman Sweatt stands with his wife in front of the Supreme Court building. Sweatt brought a case against the University of Texas Law School after being denied entrance because of his race.

the basement of a building north of the state capitol. This temporary facility, part of the new Texas State University for Negroes, would allow Sweatt to enroll within the time frame specified by the court. But Heman Sweatt was not happy. All his life he had gone to segregated schools. As a young boy, he had passed two white schools on his two-mile trek to the school for black children. Now he refused to abandon the case that might open up the white law school to blacks. Eventually he took his lawsuit all the way to the Supreme Court.

Thurgood Marshall, who would later become the first African-American justice on the Supreme Court, argued the case for Sweatt. By this time the law school's permanent buildings had opened in Houston. "They can build an exact duplicate [of the white law school]," Marshall declared, "but if it is segregated, it is unequal."[10]

McLaurin v. Oklahoma

Meanwhile, another African American had filed a discrimination case that also made its way to the Supreme Court. George McLaurin was a sixty-eight-year-old professor who taught at Langston College for black students. Although he was accepted into the University of Oklahoma's Graduate School of Education, he was not allowed to mingle with the other students. A separate section was set up for him in the classroom. He was isolated at special tables in the library and cafeteria. Not surprisingly, McLaurin found the situation intolerable. So did Thurgood Marshall, who believed McLaurin's case was another good one for the NAACP to champion.[11]

Landmark Decisions

The Supreme Court announced the *Sweatt* and *McLaurin* decisions on the very same day—June 5, 1950. In the *Sweatt* ruling, the justices declared, "We cannot find substantial equality in the educational opportunities offered white and Negro law students by the State."[12] They ordered Sweatt admitted to the University of Texas Law School.

The Court also ruled that McLaurin, "having been admitted to a state-supported graduate school, must receive the same treatment at the hands of the state as students of other races."[13]

Both men had won their cases. The Court had struck down both segregated schools and segregated treatment within schools. But the decisions were written in very specific terms. They applied only to graduate schools, and they did not overrule the "separate but equal" doctrine in all situations.[14]

Brown v. Board of Education

The *Sweatt* and *McLaurin* victories helped pave the way for another segregation case eight years later. In the fall of 1950, Reverend Oliver Brown of Topeka, Kansas, made a historic decision. He would attempt to enroll his seven-year-old daughter Linda in an all-white school. Like Sweatt and McLaurin, Brown was supported by the NAACP. "My father was recruited by his childhood friend, who at the time was legal counsel for the Topeka NAACP," recalled Linda's sister Cheryl Brown Henderson in 2003. "[My parents] joined 12 other parents as plaintiffs in this class action suit; we bear this legacy proudly."[15]

To Reverend Brown, it was a simple matter of justice. A fine school existed only four blocks from his home. Why should Linda have to walk a mile to catch a bus, then travel two more miles to school? She had the same rights as any other child to attend the nearby school. But, as expected, Linda and the other African-American children were denied entrance into the white schools. Their parents filed a lawsuit that eventually reached the Supreme Court.

Meanwhile, in other parts of the country, parents were attempting to end school segregation. The Supreme Court also received cases from Virginia, South Carolina, Delaware, and the District of Columbia. The justices decided to consider all these lawsuits together, merging them under the heading *Brown* v. *Board of Education of Topeka, Kansas*. Thurgood Marshall, who had tackled so many cases for the NAACP, took on this new case too.

Lawyers for Reverend Brown and all the other parents had two main approaches to their argument: First, evidence gathered by Kenneth Clark, a black psychologist and graduate of Harvard University, demonstrated that segregation made it hard for African-American

George McLaurin attended the Graduate School of Education at the University of Oklahoma, but he was required to sit and eat separately from the other students. He is shown here in a sociology class.

children to feel good about themselves. They had little self-esteem and thought that white children were better than they were.[16] Marshall presented the Court with a written summary of Dr. Clark's work. The second approach showed that the words "separate but equal" were meaningless. Segregated schools were never equal to white schools. One example was Clarendon County, South Carolina. While $179 was spent per year on each white student, only $43 was allotted for each black student. Class size was about twenty-eight in white schools, but forty-seven in schools for black children.[17]

On May 17, 1954, the Supreme Court handed down its ruling in what has been called "the case of the century."[18] Rendering the unanimous verdict, Chief Justice Earl Warren wrote:

> To separate [children] from others of similar age and qualifications solely because of their race generates a feeling of inferiority as to their status in the community that may affect their hearts and minds in a way unlikely ever to be undone. . . . We conclude that in the field of public education the doctrine of "separate but equal" has no place. Separate educational facilities are inherently unequal.[19]

Looking back on the case fifty years later, Cheryl Brown Henderson expressed her sense of dedication. She said, "Being the family of the namesake of this judicial turning point comes with a responsibility to teach and never let the country forget what it took for some of its citizens to be afforded their constitutional rights."[20]

A Snail's Pace

By this time, Linda Brown was eleven years old. She had advanced beyond the grade school into a junior high that had been integrated earlier. But younger children, including Cheryl, benefited from *Brown* v. *Board of Education*. They were now allowed to attend school with white students. But although the Brown decision was welcome, African Americans still had to fight for their rights. Many southern whites were angry and determined to resist change. They would do almost anything to keep black and white children in separate schools.

One example concerns the treatment of children who took part in the 1954 field test of Jonas Salk's polio vaccine. Before the *Brown* ruling, more than a million first, second, and third graders across the nation began receiving a series of three polio shots at school. In Montgomery, Alabama, however, no facilities for administering the vaccine were set up at schools for African Americans. Parents had to take their children to white schools for the shots. Then the youngsters were not allowed in the buildings. Even after the *Brown* decision in May, African-American children were forced to receive their final shots on the schools' front lawns.[21]

In 1955, the Supreme Court issued a second opinion, called *Brown II*, which stated that the integration of public schools should move forward "with all deliberate speed."[22] But what did "deliberate speed" mean? A year or ten years or longer? And what should the school boards do to achieve racially balanced schools? *Brown II* did not say.

Alabama, Georgia, and Virginia fought especially hard to resist change. They passed laws in opposition to the *Brown II* ruling. Schools in these states were directed *not* to integrate. Congress did little to force the school districts into action. One year after the second ruling, three quarters of the southerners in the House of Representatives and all but three of the senators from the southern states signed a statement called the Southern Manifesto. "We regard the decision of the Supreme Court in the school cases as a clear abuse of judicial power," they wrote.[23] They pledged to defend separate schools for black and white children. Senator Strom Thurmond even called for the impeachment of the justices.[24]

Segregationists formed Citizens' Councils in the South to "make it difficult, if not impossible, for any Negro who advocates desegregation to find and hold a job, get credit, or renew a mortgage."[25]

When nine African American students enrolled at all-white Central High School in Little Rock, Arkansas, in September 1957, angry white mobs tried to keep them out. President Dwight D. Eisenhower sent twelve hundred federal troops to ensure the students' safety. "Mob rule cannot be allowed to override the decisions of our courts," he explained in a nationally televised speech.[26] Once inside the school, the newcomers faced prejudice and jeers from some of their fellow students.

For most African-American children in the South, little changed in the years following *Brown* v. *Board of Education*. Ten years after the decision, only 2 percent of African-American children living in the South went to school with white children.[27] Little had been done to end segregation in the North either.

Not until the 1968 case of *Green* v. *School Board of New Kent County, Virginia*, would the Supreme Court finally declare that schools had an "affirmative duty" to do whatever was necessary to create integrated schools and to end racial intoler- ance.[28] According to this important ruling, "The constitutional rights of Negro school children as articulated in *Brown* permit no less than this."[29] In the meantime, one impatient observer compared the rate of progress to "an extraordinarily arthritic snail."[30]

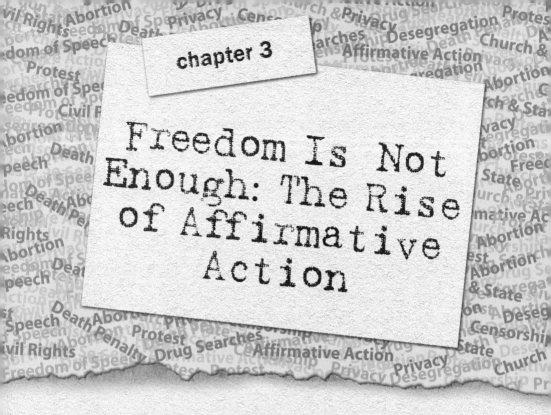

chapter 3

Freedom Is Not Enough: The Rise of Affirmative Action

African Americans were tired of waiting for their rights. On December 1, 1955, an African-American seamstress named Rosa Parks refused to give up her seat on the bus to a white man. Her arrest shocked the black community of Montgomery, Alabama, into action. Hurriedly a boycott of city buses was organized. A young, gifted minister named Martin Luther King, Jr., was named head of a new group called the Montgomery Improvement Association. Its purpose was to support the boycott.

That evening King had only twenty minutes to prepare a speech. Later he would call it "one of the most important speeches of his life."[1] Addressing a large rally, he declared, "For many years we have shown amazing patience." But there were limits to what African Americans were willing to endure. "We come here tonight," continued King, "to be saved from that patience that makes us patient with anything less than freedom and justice."[2]

For over a year, black citizens avoided Montgomery's buses. Finally the Supreme Court declared segregation on public transportation unconstitutional. Civil rights leaders felt so encouraged that they formed a new organization, the Southern Christian Leadership Conference. Led by Dr. King, the new group worked to establish racial equality.

A Stand for Equality

Surprisingly, civil rights was not considered a key issue in the presidential race of 1960.[3] Late in the campaign, however, the Democratic candidate, John F. Kennedy, helped Martin Luther King, Jr., who had been jailed for a minor traffic offense. Thanks to Kennedy's involvement, a Georgia judge freed King on bail. This may be one reason why record numbers of African Americans voted Democratic, helping Kennedy to narrowly defeat Richard Nixon.

If they were hoping for immediate and dramatic support from the president, African Americans were disappointed. President Kennedy was a practical politician. He knew he would need the votes of southern whites to ensure his reelection in four years. He did not call for immediate civil rights legislation, and he appointed several people who supported segregation to government positions.

But Kennedy realized that it was time for the United States government to get involved. On March 6, 1961, just two months after his inauguration, President John Kennedy issued a very important document—Executive Order 10925. With this mandate, he created the President's Committee on Equal Employment Opportunity. The new organization would deal with companies who worked for the government. These businesses were forbidden to "discriminate against any employee or applicant for employment because of race, creed, color, or national origin."[4] But that was not all. The businesses were also required to use "affirmative action" to make sure that everyone who worked for them or filed an application did get fair treatment. Employers had to especially encourage African Americans and other minorities to apply for jobs and promotions. Although the phrase was coined in 1935, Executive Order 10925 is usually remembered as the first use of the words "affirmative action."[5]

The Civil Rights Act of 1964

Important gains were being made toward equality for all Americans, but the rate of progress was still

28

too slow. In 1963, nine years after *Brown* v. *Board of Education*, African Americans still struggled for acceptance in colleges and universities. When two black students registered for summer classes at the University of Alabama, President Kennedy had to call out the state National Guard to guarantee their safe admission to campus. That very afternoon he discussed the situation on radio and television. "I hope that every American, regardless of where he lives, will stop and examine his conscience," the president said. He wanted broad legislation that would give "all Americans the right to be served in facilities which are open to the public—hotels, restaurants, theaters, retail stores, and similar establishments."[6] In addition, the proposed legislation called for the government to become more involved in lawsuits that fought discrimination in the schools.

President Kennedy did not live to see the passage of the bill. His assassination on November 22, 1963, shocked the nation and the world. Even while Americans were still in deep mourning, the new president Lyndon B. Johnson proclaimed Kennedy's legislation the "first priority" of his administration.[7] He considered it a fitting tribute to the slain president.[8]

The South, however, was not going to give in without a fight. Although the House of Representatives passed the bill quickly, the Senate argued for eighty-two days. Its disputes filled over six thousand pages. Finally, the senators passed the bill with a vote of 73 to 27. President Johnson signed it into law on July 2, 1964. Among other things, the bill denied federal funding to public and private organizations that discriminated against African Americans. It also gave money to help schools become integrated. Now schools had two big reasons to end segregation. The law demanded it, and federal money was available to help schools reach their goals. As a result, many schools would become integrated.

Freedom Is Not Enough

Almost a year later, President Johnson received an honorary doctorate from Howard University, a traditionally black institution of higher learning. Standing outside the library, the president shared his vision of the future of civil rights. Laws had been established to safeguard the freedom of African Americans. "But," the president told the graduating class of 1965,

> . . . freedom is not enough. . . . You do not take a person who, for years, has been hobbled by chains and liberate him, bring him up to the starting line of a race and then say, "you are free to compete with all the others," and still justly believe that you have been completely fair. . . . We seek not just freedom but opportunity. We seek not just legal equity but human ability, not just equality as a right and a theory but equality as a fact.[9]

This picture of an integrated classroom in Washington, D.C., was taken in 1957. But many schools remained segregated for years after the 1954 Brown v. Board of Education *decision.*

The president meant that new laws, however helpful, would not eliminate poverty and prejudice overnight. It would take much more than a signature on a civil rights bill to wipe out the effects of discrimination. Something more needed to be done—something to make certain that African Americans were well represented in good jobs and colleges.

Two months after his speech, Johnson signed a bill that he would call his "greatest accomplishment"—the Voting Rights Act of 1965.[10] New rules were set in place to make sure that poll taxes and literacy tests did not deprive African Americans of their right to vote. If need be, government officials could be sent into an area to help register voters and to watch over the election process.

The Invisible Milestone

Turning back to employment, Johnson spelled out what needed to be done to help African Americans get the jobs they wanted. On September 24, he issued Executive Order 11246, which called for big changes in the workforce. The heads of all government departments and agencies had to "maintain a positive program of equal employment opportunity for all civilian employees and applicants."[11] Employers also had to ensure that African Americans and other minorities had the same chance for advancement and pay raises as everyone else. From now on, no one was to have an advantage simply because he was white.

After the passionate public debates over the civil rights bill, few people took notice of the new executive order. But quietly the concept of affirmative action began to evolve. The White House itself would no longer watch over business practices. Instead that task fell to the new Office of Federal Contract Compliance in the Department of Labor. Because of this, more people could spend more time enforcing affirmative action policies. These changes are so important that journalist

Nicholas Lemann has called Executive Order 11246 "an invisible milestone."[12] It was a huge boost to affirmative action.

For two years, the Labor Department concentrated on helping minorities. Meanwhile, women were also struggling for job opportunities and equal pay. They were becoming more vocal and demanding their rights. In 1967, Johnson amended his original order with Executive Order 11375. Women were also to benefit from affirmative action. Employers were forbidden to discriminate against them in the hiring process.

The Philadelphia Plan

Thanks to Johnson's executive order, people who had a complaint against an employer could bring their case to the Labor Department for review. Soon the new department was swamped with complaints. It began to look at the numbers of minority men and of women hired by a business. If too few African Americans had jobs, that could indicate an employer was not taking affirmative measures.

Labor Department officials discovered an especially suspicious situation in Philadelphia's construction industry. The jobs were staffed almost solely by white males. In fact, minorities accounted for only one percent of membership in the union to which many construction workers belonged. Assistant Secretary of Labor Arthur

Fletcher called the industry one of the worst "offenders against equal opportunity laws" and "openly hostile toward letting blacks into their closed circle."[13] To remedy this situation, the Labor Department issued a set of guidelines called the Philadelphia Plan. These set some very specific goals for the city's building industry to meet. For example, in 1970, contractors were told to aim for a workforce in which minorities made up from 4 to 9 percent.[14]

The plan worked so well that President Richard Nixon decided to expand it beyond the construction industry and beyond Philadelphia. All businesses that made more than $50,000 working for the government and that employed at least fifty people were bound by the guidelines.[15] Goals were established to increase the number of African Americans in certain industries. Timetables were set up to meet these goals. It was no longer enough to advertise jobs widely among minorities. The government wanted results. That meant numbers.[16] Businesses had to document the percentage of African Americans and women in their workforce as a condition to keep working for the government.

Across the Nation

State and local governments began to adopt affirmative action measures of their own. Private

Legal Terms

amicus curiae—Literally, "friend of the court"; someone who files a brief in a case to which he or she is not a party but has a strong interest. Such briefs let the court benefit from the added viewpoint.

appellate court (also called court of appeals)—A court that reviews decisions of lower courts for fairness and accuracy. An appellate court can reverse a lower court's ruling.

appellant or petitioner—The person who feels the lower court made an error.

appellee or respondent—The person who won the case in the lower court.

brief—Written statement of a party's argument on one or more issues in the case.

concur—To agree with the majority in a court case.

dissent—To disagree with the majority in a court case.

majority opinion—The ruling and reasoning supported by a majority of appellate court judges in a case. **Concurring opinions** are written by judges who agree with the majority opinion but have other reasons for their views. **Dissenting opinions** are written by judges who disagree with the ruling.

precedent—A legal holding that will determine how courts decide future cases.

businesses and schools voluntarily did the same. Many whites as well as African-Americans felt that the special attention for minorities was justified. They believed that affirmative action was necessary if African Americans were to assume their rightful places in the nation's economy. Some also thought that such policies might lessen the possibility of future racial tensions. Affirmative action seemed a fair and practical way to compensate for the years of suffering and discrimination that African Americans had endured.

The rapid spread of affirmative action made many people think that the new policies were here to stay.[17] But once equality was achieved, affirmative action would no longer be necessary. It was supposed to open opportunities for minorities in education and the workforce. As more African Americans graduated from good colleges and established themselves professionally, future generations would not suffer from the disadvantages their parents and grandparents had faced. The whole goal was to help minorities to the point where they no longer needed help.

Strong and Weak Affirmative Action

Despite the growing support for affirmative action, some confusion still existed. What exactly does affirmative action mean? How much help and consideration should be given to minorities? Under what circumstances?

Basically, affirmative action policies can be applied in two main areas: education and the workforce. Each of these can be divided into two further categories: strong affirmative action and weak affirmative action. Weak affirmative action includes anything to ensure that minorities have the same opportunities as everyone else.[18] For example, a business might recruit job applications from African-American communities. A college might offer special scholarships for members of certain ethnic groups. Such measures do not guarantee a job or school admission to any particular candidate, but they foster ambition and promote diversity. In other words, weak affirmative action helps to equalize opportunities.

Champions of strong affirmative action are just as concerned with results as they are with opportunities.[19] It is not enough for schools or businesses to encourage minorities. They are required to achieve a certain racial balance in their student bodies or among their employees. Often this means reserving a certain number of jobs or class places for African Americans or members of other ethnic groups—in other words, establishing quotas that schools or businesses are required to meet. In some cases it may mean that a minority applicant is chosen for a job or for college admission over whites who seem to be more qualified.

Although weak affirmative action is generally accepted, strong affirmative action has generated a great deal of controversy and raised difficult questions. Is it fair to reserve a set number of school placements or jobs for minorities? Do they really need this kind of help? Does affirmative action lead to a more just society for everyone? People continue to debate this issue hotly.

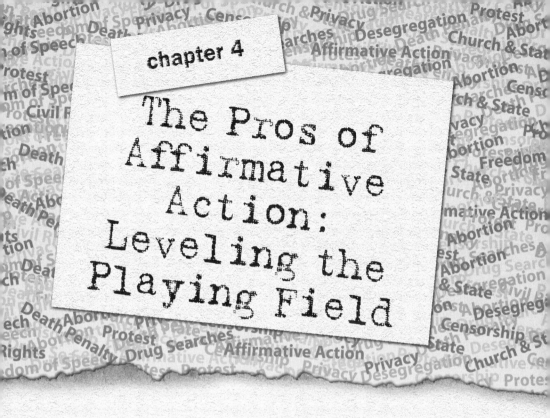

chapter 4

The Pros of Affirmative Action: Leveling the Playing Field

President Lyndon B. Johnson once compared affirmative action to sports: "Imagine a hundred yard dash. One of the two runners has his legs shackled together. He has progressed 10 yards, while the unshackled runner has gone 50 yards."[1] What should be done? the president asked. Some people might say that it is enough to unshackle the runner's legs. Then both athletes could compete freely.

Johnson pointed out that one runner was still forty yards behind the other. It was not his fault that his legs had been tied together. But it would be almost impossible for him to win the race. His opponent was halfway to the finish line, and he was just starting. Johnson thought the shackled runner should be advanced those forty yards or that the race should be started all over again. "That would be affirmative action towards equality," he concluded.[2] His analogy is sometimes described as "leveling the playing field."

Many people have agreed with Johnson. Segregation has ended, but African Americans still suffer its lingering effects. Before *Brown* v. *Board of Education*, some states spent four times as much money on white schools as on black schools.[3] Twenty-nine medical schools and forty law schools existed for white (mostly male) students in these locations. But African-American students had no choices. There was only one medical school and one law school that they could attend.[4]

Even when more colleges began admitting minorities, things did not automatically even out. Young African Americans needed the confidence to compete. They needed to believe in themselves and to dream big. But many children still attended poor elementary and high schools. They saw their parents working hard in low-paying jobs. And they still faced prejudice. Under these circumstances, it was hard for them to believe that things could really get better. President Johnson believed that affirmative action would give them hope for a brighter future.

Meanwhile, white men continued to dominate most professions. As recently as 1998, statistics

President Lyndon Johnson was a strong supporter of affirmative action. He is shown here with Thurgood Marshall, the first African-American Supreme Court justice.

showed that white males entering various jobs still received higher starting salaries than women or members of minority groups.[5] Supporters of affirmative action point out that African Americans, Hispanics, and other groups as well as women are just as capable as white males. They argue that the imbalance must be due to discrimination. According to them, affirmative action is a way to erase these inequities and bring everyone up to the same starting line.

Putting Talent to Good Use

Through affirmative action, deserving individuals have the opportunity to explore talents that might otherwise go undeveloped. Their accomplishments have a positive effect not just on minorities, but on society as a whole, say proponents.

One example of an individual who benefited from affirmative action and went on to serve the entire nation is military hero Colin Powell. Despite his bravery in Vietnam and his strong leadership skills, Powell, an African American, was not placed on a list of men for possible promotion to general in the 1970s. Clifford Alexander, who served as secretary of the Army under President Jimmy Carter, was dismayed. No African Americans at all were on the list. Alexander refused to consider the list until some African-American officers were added. Then he selected Powell to become a brigadier general. Powell went on to provide the military strategy that helped win the Gulf War and to serve as secretary of state during the first term of President George W. Bush.

Powell feels that affirmative action is necessary to ensure that all children have the same chance to develop their abilities.[6] "I believe race should be a factor among many other factors in determining the makeup of a student body of a university," he has said.[7]

Another outstanding beneficiary of affirmative

action is Harvard law professor and author Charles J. Ogletree, Jr. No one in his family had ever attended college. "Without affirmative action," Ogletree has written, "I would never have applied to, and certainly would not have attended, Stanford."[8]

Ruth Simmons, the president of Brown University and the first African American to head an Ivy League school, would like to see affirmative action broadened. "Discrimination endures, that is undeniable," she has stated.[9] In her view, students from impoverished backgrounds, regardless of their race, should be given special consideration in college admissions. She has called affirmative action "one of the most far-reaching and important government actions of our time."[10]

Supporters point out that thanks to the help affirmative action provides, minorities have established themselves in medicine, law, education, business, science, and other fields. Seeing a black newscaster on television, or being treated by a black doctor, lets African-American youngsters know that they can grow up to have good jobs too. It encourages them to plan for their futures and to work hard.

Looking Toward the Past

Some people view affirmative action as a way to make up for past wrongs. Because African

Americans suffered so much in the past, it is only fair that they be given special consideration today, these people say. Affirmative action can help members of minority groups gain some of the advantages that would have been theirs if their ancestors had enjoyed their full rights as citizens. These advantages include good jobs, economic security, and leadership positions in society. According to supporters, slavery, segregation, and racial prejudice in the past more than justify the affirmative action programs that attempt to help African Americans today. This is called a backward-looking argument because it looks to the past to justify affirmative action.[11]

Looking to the Future

The signers of the Declaration wrote that "all men are created equal" and have the same right to "life, liberty, and the pursuit of happiness." But historically this promise of freedom has not held true for African Americans, for other minorities, and for women desiring careers outside the home. Supporters of affirmative action say that it aims to create a future society in which all Americans can live the ideals expressed by the founding fathers. This is called a forward-looking argument.[12]

In addition, supporters point out that it is extremely important for African Americans, Hispanics, American Indians, and women to work as lawyers, doctors, teachers, airplane pilots, engineers, newscasters, and in other professions. This helps break down old stereotypes that held that only a certain class of people was capable of filling such positions. Employers and the general public come to think of certain groups differently, to appreciate their capabilities and talents. In this way, the argument goes, affirmative action has a positive ripple effect that spreads outward from the people who have received special consideration. For example, when white children have a chance to study from black teachers, they learn more than just math or history. They learn tolerance and respect too.

What happens in the classroom also happens in society as a whole. Individuals like Colin Powell and Ruth Simmons are as inspiring to white citizens as they are to African Americans. So is Kim Keenan, an African-American woman who has held many important positions in the legal profession. "As long as I can walk into a room and people are surprised that I actually exist," she says, "then we need affirmative action."[13]

Such policies continue the integration of society that began with the civil rights movement. Supporters say that affirmative action provides a needed diversity in education and business. This creates a more just society in which people look at each other as individuals rather than merely members of a particular ethnic group.

Opponents, on the other hand, say that affirmative action does the opposite. It makes racial classifications more important than individual accomplishment. These opponents champion a society in which race has no place in school or job decisions. Point by point, they attempt to refute the arguments for affirmative action.

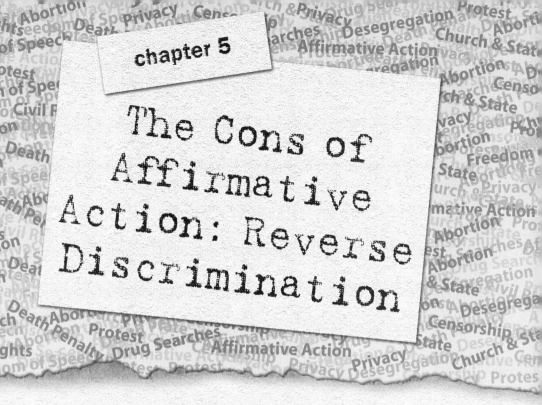

chapter 5

The Cons of Affirmative Action: Reverse Discrimination

Opponents of affirmative action argue that the law should be "color-blind." Justice John Harlan used these words in 1896 when he opposed the Supreme Court decision that allowed separate sections for whites and blacks on public transportation. He meant that laws should not discriminate against African Americans in any way. Every person, no matter the color of his skin, deserves the same treatment.

According to some people, "color blindness" works in two directions. On the one hand, members of minority groups have legal protection from discrimination. On the other hand, they are not entitled to special consideration because of their race or ethnic background. Affirmative action makes race a very big issue when it gives advantages to minorities that it denies to whites. Instead of promoting equality and tolerance, it may actually increase tensions between the races, opponents of affirmative action say.[1]

The Equal Protection of the Fourteenth Amendment to the Constitution spells out certain basic rights:

No state shall make or enforce any law which shall abridge the privileges or immunities of citizens of the United States; nor shall any State deprive any person of life, liberty, or property, without due process of law; nor deny to any person within its jurisdiction the equal protection of the laws.

Adopted in 1868, the Fourteenth Amendment was conceived as a safeguard to the rights of African Americans newly freed from slavery. However, it also protects the rights of every American, regardless of color. Opponents say that affirmative action policies, which favor one race over the other, violate the Fourteenth Amendment because such policies do not treat all citizens equally. This means that race, ethnic background, or gender should never be a factor in college admissions or in the job market.

The Most Qualified Candidate

According to those who oppose affirmative action, businesses and schools should choose the most qualified applicants for available jobs or for next year's freshman class. Affirmative action interferes with that selection process. For example, good grades, high test scores, and personal recommendations are used to predict success in college. When college admissions officers take race into consideration, the most qualified applicants do not always get chosen. Someone with high grades may lose out to someone with lower grades. Someone who did well on college entrance tests may be rejected in favor of someone who made lower scores. This is not fair to white students, who are penalized because of their race. In fact, this situation is sometimes called "reverse discrimination." Critics argue that discrimination is just as wrong when it harms whites as when it harms blacks.

But what about less qualified students who get into college or less qualified applicants who get the job? Are they harmed in any way? Some opponents of affirmative action claim that they are. The student with the lower test scores and poorer grades may not be able to compete with classmates who have stronger academic records.[2] Minority students who benefited from affirmative action may find themselves behind in math or science or writing skills. They may have to struggle harder to pass their classes. Some statistics indicate that the college dropout rate for African Americans is much higher than it is for white students.[3] One explanation put forth by critics is that poorly prepared students are being admitted through affirmative action programs.[4] In the long run, they have been hurt by their enrollment in schools for which they were not truly qualified.

The public too may suffer if less capable applicants are chosen to fill important positions. This is especially true when safety is involved. Arthur Hu, who has studied affirmative action and written for the magazine *Asian Weekly*, summed up this position with a question: "Would you fly in an airplane from a company whose motto is, 'We Put Diversity First'?"[5] Whatever their feelings about affirmative action, most people would respond with an emphatic no.

The Neediest Individuals

Not all African Americans or members of other minority groups need help. Many black families are well off enough to live in nice neighborhoods and to give their sons and daughters enrichment experiences such as summer camp or music or tennis lessons. The children do not suffer from attending poor schools or living in cramped, segregated communities. The parents have the leisure and background to help the children with their homework and to encourage their ambitions.

Opponents contend that minority students from middle-class or affluent families are well able to compete with white students for admissions to top schools. But colleges may find the more privileged individuals to be better qualified academically than students from poor families. They have had more opportunities and perhaps suffered less discrimination. Should they be given an advantage over white students when applying to college or white applicants when seeking a job? Opponents say they should not. Yet schools and companies that practice affirmative action may end up choosing the person who has already had the most advantages. They are not really the people that affirmative action is meant to benefit, say opponents. According to such critics, affirmative action does little for those who need the help most.[6]

Looking to the Past

Those who support affirmative action point to the horrible injustices endured by African Americans and members of other minority groups. Simple justice demands compensation for the ills they have suffered. However, opponents of affirmative action argue that this is not so. Many of those who were denied an equal education, the right to vote, or simply the freedom to choose their seat on a train or bus are no longer living. Others are very elderly. It is too late to help them. Affirmative action cannot change history. Opponents say that affirmative action should not be a means to remedy past wrongs.[7] All that can be done today is to make sure that African Americans enjoy the same rights as everyone else. They do not deserve special privileges just because people have been hurt in the past.

Many people guilty of discrimination have also died. It is too late for them to make up for what they did. But large numbers of people alive today have never taken part in any form of discrimination. Their ancestors may not even have lived in the United States during the worst periods of injustice. Opponents claim that affirmative action makes them pay for deeds they never committed.

Is Affirmative Action Demeaning?

Affirmative action causes some individuals to take a cynical view of African-American achievement, say opponents. African Americans who rise to leadership positions in industry, education, or other fields may not be seen for their outstanding qualities and expertise. Instead, some members of the white majority will view their success as entirely dependent on their race.[8] This attitude leads to tension in the workplace and in society. Instead of improving, relations between the races could get worse.

Certain people find the whole notion of affirmative action belittling to African Americans. Ward Connerly, a prominent African-American businessman, told the *Sacramento Bee* in 1991, "I'm opposed to [affirmative action]. For me, it's the ultimate insult. I don't need any brownie points from anybody. I don't want any from anybody."[9] In 1993, he became a member of the board of regents

Ward Connerly, an African American who opposes affirmative action, led a movement to end racial preferences at the University of California.

of the University of California. Soon he realized that some minority students with lower grades and test scores were admitted over white applicants who had better academic records. This bothered Connerly deeply. "We operated on the presumption that if you were black or Hispanic, you would never be able to compete," he recalled. "To even raise that question was sort of being like the skunk at the picnic."[10]

Largely through Connerly's efforts, the regents decided to end racial preferences at the University of California. There would be no more "set-aside" programs to reserve a certain number of places solely for African Americans. Connerly and other opponents of affirmative action believe that minority students deserve a better education in elementary school and in high school. What they really want to do is "level the playing field" long before college. In a society where all children enjoy the same advantages, there will be no need for affirmative action, they say.

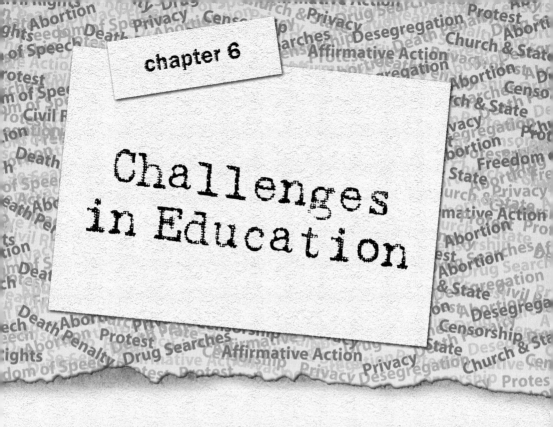

chapter 6

Challenges in Education

In the 1970s, the number of affirmative action programs mushroomed. All over the country, colleges began to use race as a factor when deciding who would be admitted to the freshman class. As more African Americans, Hispanics, and other minorities were accepted into schools, fewer places were left for white males. Some of these rejected young men, however, seemed better qualified than the candidates who gained admission. They had better grades and entrance test scores. What was the point of their hard work, they wondered, if someone less well prepared for challenging academics was chosen before they were? One of the people who asked this question was an applicant to medical school named Allan Bakke.

Thwarted Ambition

In his early thirties, Bakke was older than many of the other applicants to medical school. He already had a master's degree in mechanical engineering and had served with the Marine Corps in Vietnam. Like all fighting men, Bakke saw a great deal of suffering during his time in Vietnam. He decided to become a doctor to help others. When Bakke returned to the United States, he studied biology and chemistry and volunteered in an emergency room. "More than anything else in the world, I want to study medicine," he wrote on his application to the University of California at Davis (UCD).[1]

Bakke had received outstanding scores on his medical school entrance tests. But, to his disappointment, he was not offered one of the one hundred available slots in the first-year class in 1973. The next year he applied again, only to receive another rejection.

Bakke believed that he would have been accepted if it were not for one thing. Sixteen positions in the freshman class were reserved for minorities. These students were not held to the same high standards as the general pool of applicants. Test scores and grades that were not acceptable for white applicants were considered all right for minorities. In fact, the two groups were never even compared. A separate committee was set up to judge the qualifications of minority

Getting a Case to the Supreme Court

People who want their cases heard before the Supreme Court face an uphill battle. The majority of the cases that are appealed to the Court are not accepted for review. In a few instances, however, the justices grant certiorari. This means they are willing to hear the case. Once a case is accepted, a strict procedure is followed:

(1) During oral arguments, lawyers for both the appellant (the person bringing the suit) and appellee (the person who answers the suit) present their side of the story. There is no argument about the facts of the case. The important issue is whether or not an action or policy violates the Constitution. No witnesses are called, but the justices may interrupt lawyers with questions at any time.

(2) After the oral arguments are over, the justices may take many months to reach a decision. At least five of the nine justices must support a position for it to become a ruling.

(3) One justice writes the majority opinion, which explains the reasoning behind a decision. Sometimes other justices write agreeing or concurring opinions. They have something they want to add to the decision—perhaps a line of reasoning that was not covered in the majority opinion.

(4) Justices who disagree with the majority may also write opinions explaining their views.

students. To Bakke's way of thinking, this was discrimination. He decided to sue the university to gain admission into medical school.

Lower Court Rulings

The decision of the California Superior Court satisfied neither Bakke nor the University of California. The court decided that the university's minority admission program was unfair to white applicants. It violated the Civil Rights Act of 1964, the Fourteenth Amendment, and the California state constitution. However, the court did not agree that Bakke would have been admitted to medical school if it were not for the minority program. Other factors, such as his age or his interviews, might have prevented his acceptance. Although the university's affirmative action policy was overturned, the court did not order Bakke's admission into medical school.

The California Supreme Court proved more favorable to Bakke. It upheld the ruling against the minority admissions program. More importantly to Bakke, it required the medical school to admit him. Officials at Davis, however, still believed their position was correct. They decided to appeal to the United States Supreme Court.

Meanwhile, Allan Bakke's hands were tied. In November 1976, Supreme Court Justice William Rehnquist overrode the lower court order that

Bakke be admitted to medical school. If the Supreme Court declined the case, the order would go back into effect, and Bakke could start his studies. But if the Court did hear the case, Bakke's future would have to wait on its decision.

Record Turnout

On February 19, 1977, the Supreme Court granted certiorari in the *Regents of the University of California* v. *Bakke*. By this time, Bakke was almost thirty-eight years old. Most students began medical school in their twenties. Bakke had little time to spare.

All over the country people discussed and debated the *Bakke* case. Fifty-eight *amicus curiae* (friend of the court) briefs were filed—more than the Supreme Court had received in any other case. Forty-two of these briefs agreed with the university's position, while sixteen championed Allan Bakke's cause.[2] President Jimmy Carter felt that even the government should get involved. His administration decided to file an *amicus* brief supporting affirmative action.

Hundreds of people crowded into the Supreme Court to hear oral arguments on October 12, 1977. But hundreds of other people had to be turned away. The one person noticeably absent was Allan Bakke himself. His lawyer, Reynold Colvin, explained that Bakke wanted to distance himself from the press. That would simply not be possible if he attended oral arguments.[3]

Three Lawyers Weigh In

Usually two positions are heard during oral arguments. However, in the *Bakke* case, three lawyers presented three views. First, Harvard professor Archibald Cox, a former solicitor general of the United States, spoke for the university. He explained that very few African Americans were able to attend medical school. The only way to increase their numbers, he declared, was through affirmative action.

> The answer the Court gives will determine, perhaps for decades, whether members of those minorities are to have the kind of meaningful access to higher education in the professions which universities have accorded them in recent years, or are to be reduced to the trivial numbers which they were prior to the adoption of minority admissions programs.[4]

Cox concluded his arguments by stating that the Fourteenth Amendment does not forbid "race-conscious" programs as long as they are not intended to do harm and they may help undo the effects of many years of discrimination.

The second speaker, Wade H. McCree, Jr., was the current solicitor general of the United States. He had fifteen minutes to present the government's position. Referring to the example once used by

President Johnson, he said that minorities had to be brought to "the starting line."[5] Racism continued to exist, and the way to deal with it was through affirmative action.

Finally, Bakke's lawyer, Reynold Colvin, spoke. "Allan Bakke's position is that he has a right," he declared, "and that right is not to be discriminated against by reason of his race. And that's what brings Allan Bakke to this Court."[6]

A Case That Never Got Decided

It was a tough case for the justices to decide. Although this was not the first time a school had been sued over affirmative action, the Supreme Court had no prior rulings, or precedents, on which to base its judgment. In 1971, a young man named Marco deFunis had taken the law school at the University of Washington to court for failing to admit him.

The law school *had*, however, accepted thirty-six minority candidates, most of whom had lower test scores and poorer grades than deFunis did. A victory in the lower court allowed deFunis to enroll in the law school. By the time the case reached the Supreme Court in 1974, he was close to graduation. The Court heard oral arguments but decided that the case was moot, or no longer relevant. No ruling was issued.[7]

This meant that the *Bakke* case would be the

Court's first major ruling on affirmative action in higher education. Its verdict would affect colleges and universities all over the country.

Four Justices Support Bakke

On June 28, 1978, eight months after oral arguments, the Supreme Court justices were ready to announce their ruling. But they had been sharply divided in their reasoning. Four justices (John Paul Stevens, Warren Burger, Potter Stewart, and William Rehnquist) believed that racial quotas such as those the Davis medical school had used violated the Civil Rights Act of 1964. There was not any need to look beyond this statute to the Constitution. According to these justices, the ruling of the California Supreme Court should be upheld, and Bakke should be admitted to medical school immediately.

Four Justices Support the University

Some members of the court, however, saw the *Bakke* case in a different light. Justices William Brennan, Thurgood Marshall, Byron White, and Harry Blackmun felt that the university's affirmative action program did not violate either the Civil Rights Act or the Equal Protection Clause of the Fourteenth Amendment. There was a difference, they argued, between taking race into account to harm people and taking race into account to help people. The medical school's affirmative action program aimed to undo the effects of past prejudice. It gave minority applicants opportunities that had been previously denied to them.

The justices felt that several things were required for an affirmative action program to be considered constitutional. (1) There must be no "presumption that one race is inferior to another."[8] (2) The program had to fulfill an important purpose. (3) Hardships must not be placed on "those least well represented in the political process."[9] Judged by these criteria, UCD's affirmative action program was perfectly permissible.

Justice Blackmun explained his reasoning bluntly.

> In order to get beyond racism, we must first take account of race. There is no other way. And in order to treat some persons equally, we must treat them differently. We cannot—we dare not—let the Equal Protection Clause perpetuate [continue] racial supremacy.[10]

Justice Powell in the Middle

The Court was split 4 to 4. But Justice Lewis Powell did not belong to either group. He saw the danger to Bakke's rights, but he also felt that affirmative action was important and necessary. Because of his views, Powell was in a position to cast the deciding vote.[11]

Like the other justices, he had gone over four arguments the university had used to defend its affirmative action program: (1) lessening the effects of earlier discrimination; (2) increasing the number of minority doctors; (3) making medical care more available to minority communities; and (4) creating a more diverse student body.

After careful consideration, Powell dismissed the first three arguments. He said that the university itself had not discriminated. It was not up to the school to fix discrimination that had been practiced by society in general. As for the second point, schools did not have the right to set goals for how many minority doctors there should be. The third point was certainly valid. It was important to make medical care available to communities where there was little or none. But more minority doctors would not necessarily do the job. After all, some minority doctors might decide not to practice in ethnic communities, while some white doctors might choose to do so.

Strict Scrutiny

The fourth point, the importance of educational diversity, was the only one that Justice Powell found convincing. However, unlike the four justices who supported the university, Powell felt that affirmative action had to satisfy the standards of strict scrutiny. This meant that first, there had to be a "compelling state interest." Second, the affirmative action program had to be "narrowly tailored" to address only that interest and nothing more. It must attempt to fix a specific problem and not go beyond it.

Powell agreed that the case for educational diversity was indeed "compelling." But he also felt that UCD's quota system did more than it was supposed to do. It should be possible to achieve a diverse student body without reserving a set number of places for minorities and lessening the chances of qualified white applicants. In other words, the program was not "narrowly tailored."

Landmark Ruling

In announcing the opinion of the Court, Powell declared that racial quotas were illegal. This was a victory for Allan Bakke. He could attend medical school at last. But Powell also spoke for a different majority when he said that colleges could use race as a factor in deciding whom to admit as long as they did not set rigid quotas. This part of the decision upheld the university's position that affirmative action did not violate civil rights. Looking back on his career ten years later, Powell would call *Bakke* "his most important opinion."[12]

Despite the qualified approval of affirmative action, Justice Thurgood Marshall was deeply

Allan Bakke gets ready to receive his medical degree. The Supreme Court held that he should be admitted to medical school at the University of California. But it also said that schools could consider race as one factor in deciding whom to admit.

disappointed by the outcome. Although affirmative action was held constitutional as a means to achieve racially balanced student bodies, it was not ruled an acceptable way to remedy past discrimination.[13] In his dissenting opinion, Marshall wrote:

> It must be remembered that, during most of the past 200 years, the Constitution as interpreted by this Court did not prohibit the most ingenious [tricky] and pervasive [widespread] forms of discrimination against the Negro. Now, when a state acts to remedy the effects of that legacy of

discrimination, I cannot believe that this same Constitution stands as a barrier.[14]

Both sides had gained and both had lost in the *Bakke* decision. Those who opposed affirmative action were glad to see Bakke admitted to school. And those who supported affirmative action applauded the ruling that special consideration could be given to certain racial categories. Because the Supreme Court gave a mixed message, more confusion was bound to arise.

Wygant v. Jackson Board of Education

Teachers as well as students were affected by affirmative action. Throughout the country, school districts strove for diversity in their faculties. School officials in Jackson, Michigan, felt that hiring minority teachers was a good way to ease racial tension among the students. Like the board of Piscataway, New Jersey, the Jackson school board believed that the accomplishments of minority teachers would show all students that hard work pays off and that people of different races can work together successfully.

There was only one complication. Sometimes teachers had to be laid off for financial reasons. Usually teachers who had been with a school district longest (those with the most seniority) would not have to worry about losing their jobs. However, this meant that newly hired minority teachers might be the first to be laid off. To solve the problem, the school board developed a plan to ensure that a set number of minority teachers kept their jobs when layoffs became necessary.[15] This number was chosen so that the faculty would reflect the diversity of the student body. However, there were many more minority students than minority teachers. The school board was in a bind. Based on its policy, some teachers with seniority would surely have to be laid off.

In the school years 1976–1977 and 1981–1982, the school board was forced to let some teachers go. As expected, some minority teachers kept their jobs while white teachers with more seniority were laid off. This did not seem fair to the white teachers. They decided to challenge the school board in court. Since Wendy Wygant was the first name on the list of petitioners (the teachers who were bringing suit), the case became known as *Wygant v. Jackson Board of Education*. It went all the way to the Supreme Court.

In 1982, the District Court decided in favor of the school board. Administrators were trying to provide role models for minority students and lessen discrimination in society. These important goals justified making race a factor in laying off teachers. The Court of Appeals for the Sixth Circuit agreed with the lower court.

Once again, the Supreme Court was sharply divided. In a 5–4 decision, issued May 19, 1986, the Court reversed the lower court rulings and decided in favor of the teachers who had been laid off. Unless the school district had been guilty of discrimination in hiring (and the Court did not believe that it was), race should not be used as a factor in deciding which teachers to keep.

In its opinion, the Court also said that there was a big difference between using race as a factor in the hiring process and using race when it came to layoffs.[16] If a person is not hired for one job, there are others that he can apply for. However, it is very difficult to lose a job one already has. Even if a person is laid off in the name of racial integration, it is a huge price to pay. The Court recognized that the school board's goals were important. But making race part of the layoff process placed an unfair burden on certain individuals.

In other words, the board's plan did too much and demanded too great a sacrifice from innocent men and women. Future affirmative action programs would have to be carefully structured to remedy specific injustices, not cause further injustices. The general goal of lessening discrimination in society could not be used to justify affirmative action.

Hopwood v. Texas

In 1992, Cheryl Hopwood, who had applied to the University of Texas School of Law, found herself in the same position that Allan Bakke had protested fourteen years earlier. She was rejected by a school that made special allowances for minorities in the admissions process. Hopwood had worked hard during college. Although she had been accepted at Princeton University for her undergraduate years, she had not been able to afford tuition. Instead she attended community colleges and a California state university. She maintained a high grade point average, had a part-time job, and became part of the Big Sisters program. Didn't she deserve the same advantages that minority applicants received?

Cheryl Hopwood and three other disappointed white applicants decided to challenge the university's policy in court. They claimed that if they had been minority candidates, they would easily have gained acceptance into the law school. This was another instance of "reverse discrimination," they said. The rights guaranteed to them by the Equal Protection Clause of the Fourteenth Amendment had been violated.

The district court gave a mixed message to those debating the fate of affirmative action. Although the court agreed that Hopwood had been denied her rights, it also ruled that the law school could continue to make race a factor in selecting students. Hopwood and her co-petitioners were not admitted into the school. Rather they were allowed to apply again without additional fees.

A disappointed Hopwood took her claim to the Fifth Circuit of Appeals. In a stunning reversal, the court declared "that the law school may not use race as a factor in law school admissions."[17] The decision would apply only in the Fifth Circuit's jurisdiction that included Texas, Louisiana, and Mississippi. "It's not a very big deal right now to anyone outside the 5th Circuit," said John Jeffries of the University of Virginia Law School. "If applied nationwide it would be a . . . very big deal indeed."[18]

That is exactly what opponents of affirmative action hoped would happen. They wanted the ban on affirmative action to cover the entire country. But only a Supreme Court ruling could extend the ban on racial preferences to other states. Supporters of affirmative action looked for a different outcome. After all, the *Hopwood* decision contradicted the *Bakke* ruling that said race *could* be used as one of several factors in school admissions. Wouldn't the Supreme Court want to hold the Fifth Circuit to the principles set forth in *Bakke*? But in June 1996, the Supreme Court declined to hear the case. Affirmative action had effectively ended in public schools in the Fifth Circuit. If colleges and universities wished to maintain racially diverse student bodies, they had to find other ways to do so.

An Alternative to Affirmative Action?

What could be done to encourage minority students to apply to college and then to help them gain admission? The Texas legislature came up with a plan. Any student who graduated in the top 10 percent of his or her high school class would automatically be accepted into a public university. The legislators believed that this would help achieve a racial balance in the colleges. There was a practical reason for their view. In many areas of Texas, ethnic or racial groups clustered together in neighborhoods. Since students usually went to schools near their homes, this tended to make the high schools segregated too.

The Ten Percent Plan, which took effect September 1, 1997, guaranteed that the upper 10 percent of students in every high school—wherever the neighborhood—would be accepted into a public college. Top students in predominantly black or Hispanic high schools had the same chance to attend a Texas state university as students from high schools that were mostly white. "The top 10 percent bill works because there are still racially identifiable schools in the state of Texas," said a university admissions director in a 2002 interview. "It wouldn't work in a state where this is not true."[19]

Some people, however, question how effective the Ten Percent Plan is—even in places like Texas. As of 2002, minorities were still underrepresented based on their numbers in the general population. Critics of the plan point out that colleges still need to actively recruit minority students and make certain they know about the plan. They may also have to provide financial aid.[20] And what about graduate programs or law or medical schools? How are they to maintain a healthy racial mix? The Ten Percent Plan only works for college admissions. It is useless at higher levels.

Another argument against the plan sounds very similar to those sometimes made against affirmative action. The best students do not always get into the top schools.[21] Those who attend academically strong high schools may not make it into the top 10 percent of their graduating class, yet they may be better qualified than the top 10 percent of students from less demanding schools. To many people, this seems unfair.

Taxman v. Piscataway Again

Fairness is also at the heart of the lawsuit Sharon Taxman brought against the Piscataway School

Board. By the time she lost her job in 1989, the pendulum had begun to swing away from affirmative action. Taxman had lost her job because she was white. Debra Williams, her African-American colleague, kept her job because she was black. It looked as if the Supreme Court would make an important ruling on this case. Based on past decisions, such as *Wygant*, there seemed little doubt that the Court would rule in favor of Taxman.

Supporters of affirmative action were worried. The Court had already established strict scrutiny as the standard for judging affirmative action. This meant that (1) there had to be a compelling state interest; and (2) the remedy had to be limited in scope—narrowly tailored—to deal with very specific situations. Might the Court add further restrictions that would make it almost impossible for affirmative action to survive? "We felt certain it would be a death blow to affirmative action, not just in Piscataway or New Jersey, but nationwide," explained Donald K. Tucker of the New Jersey Black Issues Convention.[22]

Tucker's group was part of a larger Washington organization known as the Black Leadership Forum. This association of national civil rights groups decided to see if they could settle the case before it reached the Supreme Court. Sharon Taxman was asking for a great deal of money in lost salary and damages. The Black Leadership Forum raised $308,500 that could be used to help the school board pay Taxman the sum she demanded.[23]

But would the current board members accept it? They felt their predecessors had done nothing wrong in handling Taxman's layoff. But they also knew their chances of winning the case were slim. The decision was a tough one. Their debate lasted late into the night. Finally, in a 5–3 decision, the school board voted to take the money. Sharon Taxman was paid $433,500, and the case was withdrawn from the Supreme Court.

Many people applauded the decision, including the Reverend Reginald Jackson, the executive director of the Black Ministers' Council of New Jersey. "While it was a fight worth fighting, it's a question of what chance do you take of doing so much damage?" he said.[24] On the other hand, board member Anne Thomas felt that the case was dropped too easily. "I feel we could have won the case, and the argument that it's going to end affirmative action because we would lose the case automatically doesn't hold water with me," she declared. "Education is the thing that would have made a difference. . . . Now we'll never know."[25]

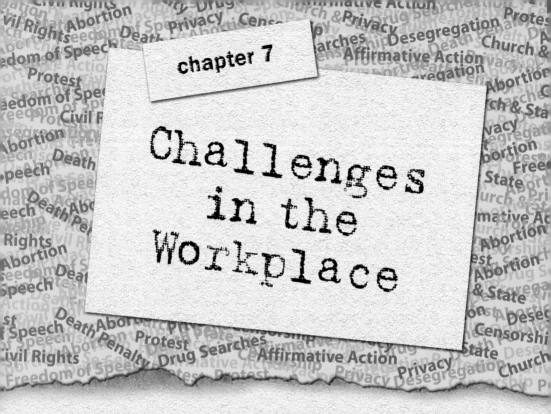

chapter 7

Challenges in the Workplace

Schools were not the only places struggling "to level the playing field." Businesses and government agencies had to make sure that they did not discriminate against minorities in hiring or promotions. Even something that seemed harmless, such as requiring a high school education for certain jobs, might be considered suspicious. That was the situation with an important case reviewed by the Supreme Court in 1979, *Griggs* v. *Duke Power Company*. The North Carolina company required certain tests as well as a high school diploma for its higher paying jobs. Willie Griggs and other petitioners claimed this was not fair. They believed that people who had not graduated from high school could perform the jobs just as well as those who had. But because fewer African Americans had completed high school, they were eliminated from the best jobs.

In 1971, the Supreme Court agreed, overruling the finding of the lower appeals court. Writing the majority opinion, Chief Justice Warren Burger pointed out that a practice can seem harmless and still discriminate. The key, he said, was business necessity. Anything that eliminated African Americans or other minorities had to be an absolutely necessary requirement for the job. If the employer could not prove this, he was in violation of the Civil Rights Act of 1964.[1]

Whether or not Duke Power meant to discriminate, their practices were holding back a whole category of people capable of doing the jobs from which they were barred. For this reason, Duke's educational requirement would have to go. Soon the *Griggs* decision would broaden the whole concept of job discrimination and affect businesses across the country.

What About the Rights of Nonminorities?

The *Griggs* case was concerned with fairness to African Americans, but throughout the 1970s and 1980s, the Supreme Court faced a series of cases that turned that situation around. Businesses all over the country had adopted affirmative action programs. Job candidates who were not members of minority groups believed that their rights were being violated by the preferences given African Americans and Hispanics.

In *United Steelworkers* v. *Weber*, the Court had to decide whether a training program in which half the positions were reserved for African Americans violated the Civil Rights Act. The 50 percent quota had been established to remedy a situation in Gramercy, Louisiana, where almost no African-American employees held skilled jobs with the steel company.[2] Brian Weber, a white man who had been turned down for the new training program, charged discrimination. He felt that the Civil Rights Act of 1964 should protect him from being passed over on the basis of race. In 1979, however, the Supreme Court upheld the legality of the affirmative action program. Justice Brennan wrote:

> It would be ironic indeed if a law triggered by a Nation's concern over centuries of racial injustice . . . constituted the first legislative prohibition of all voluntary, private, race-conscious efforts to abolish traditional patterns of racial segregation and hierarchy.[3]

One year later, in *Fullilove* v. *Klutznick*, the Court again faced the issue of racial preferences. The case concerned a law enacted by Congress that specified 15 percent of the public works undertaken by the government to go to qualified minority contractors. The white owner of a heating and air conditioning company claimed that the law had cost him money. So did several other companies. What was the use of submitting the lowest bid for a job if the work was going to go to a minority company anyway? But the Supreme Court, in a 6–3 decision, refused to interfere with the workings of Congress. The set-aside program was not declared unconstitutional.[4]

Affirmative action could help women as well as minorities. In *Johnson* v. *Transportation Agency, Santa Clara County, Calif.*, Paul Johnson claimed he had been passed over for a road dispatcher's job in favor of a woman who was not as qualified as he was. Once again, the Supreme Court's vote was close. In 1987, in a 5–4 decision, they ruled that the transportation department was entitled to use affirmative action when minorities or women were underrepresented among the employees.[5] In a dissenting opinion, Justice Antonin Scalia protested that "the goal of a discrimination-free society" was not the same thing as "proportionate representation by race and by sex in the workplace."[6] In other words, there could be many reasons why women or minorities were not well represented in a company. Small numbers did not necessarily mean that discrimination occurred.

A Turning Point: *Richmond* v. *Croson Company*

The city of Richmond, Virginia, however, was very concerned with numbers. During a five-year period (1978–1983), minority businesses had received less than $1 million worth of business from the city. White-owned companies, on the other hand, had received over $124 million.[7] In 1983, the city council passed an ordinance requiring all construction companies who received contracts from the city to allot, or subcontract, 30 percent of the work to minority businesses. These secondary businesses could be located anywhere in the country. The ordinance meant that when the primary company needed to hire plumbers or electricians or carpenters for the job, minority businesses would have a good chance to be chosen.[8]

Council members believed that the Supreme Court's ruling in *Fullilove* v. *Klutznick* had established the legality of quotas as a means to remedy discrimination. But soon they were challenged by the Croson Company, an Ohio business, which had received a contract to put stainless steel plumbing faucets and pipes in the Richmond jail. When Croson claimed he could not find a minority business from which to buy the plumbing fixtures, his contract was canceled. Croson decided to sue the city. He said his

Fourteenth Amendment rights had been violated and that there was no compelling government interest for Richmond's policy of quotas.

In 1989, the Supreme Court struck down Richmond's affirmative action plan. The justices ruled that the city's quota plan did not pass the strict scrutiny standard. The program was not narrowly tailored enough. There were other, better ways to deal with a problem of past discrimination in the building industry.[9] A turning point had been reached. The Court was now saying that past discrimination in society was too vague a charge on which to build an affirmative action program.[10] And even if Richmond had proved that discrimination was specifically practiced in the building industry, the city had not attempted to address the issue in a race-neutral manner.

Justice Blackmun was deeply dismayed by the ruling. In his dissenting opinion, he wrote:

> I never thought that I would live to see the day when the city of Richmond, Virginia, the cradle of the Old Confederacy, sought on its own, within a narrow confine, to lessen the stark impact of persistent discrimination. But Richmond, to its great credit, acted. Yet this Court, the supposed bastion [stronghold] of equality, strikes down Richmond's efforts as though discrimination had never existed or was not demonstrated in this particular litigation [lawsuit].[11]

Are Figures Enough? *Wards Cove Packing Company* v. *Atonio*

Another important case came to the Supreme Court the same year as *Croson*. A serious racial imbalance existed at the Wards Cove Packing Company in Alaska. Two minority groups, native Alaskans and Filipinos, filled most of the jobs in the cannery where they packed salmon. White workers occupied almost all of the higher paying office jobs. Did this mean that the Wards Cove Company discriminated?

Not necessarily, said the Supreme Court. The justices ruled that there could be many other reasons why the minority employees were held back. Maybe they did not have the education or the qualifications for office work. Maybe those who did qualify were looking for jobs elsewhere. Employment figures alone did not provide enough evidence for the Supreme Court.[12]

This opinion reversed the

People have strong feelings on both sides of the affirmative action debate. Here demonstrators in New York protest the Bakke *decision.*

Court's previous decision in the *Griggs* case. Then the Court *had* accepted racial imbalance as proof of discrimination. Now the burden of proof had shifted from the employer to the employee. No longer did a company have to prove that it did not discriminate. Instead, workers with complaints had to prove that it did.[13]

When Federal Laws Are Involved: *Metro Broadcasting* v. *FCC*

The *Wards Cove* decision applied to private businesses. But what happened when the government was involved? Were federal regulations designed to favor minorities constitutional? That was the issue the Court faced one year later in *Metro Broadcasting* v. *Federal Communications Commission (FCC)*. According to FCC policies enacted by Congress, African Americans and other minorities received special consideration when applying for broadcasting licenses. The hope was that more minority ownership of television and radio stations would lead to greater diversity in the programs available to the general public.

Although the *Croson* decision had struck down racial preferences, the Supreme Court ruled that the FCC was justified in giving special consideration to minority broadcasters. Once again, the Court was sharply divided. "It is of overriding significance in these cases," wrote Justice Brennan for the majority, "that the FCC's minority ownership programs have been specially approved—indeed, mandated—by Congress. In light of that fact, this Court owes appropriate deference to Congress's judgment."[14] The majority of the justices felt that intermediate scrutiny (a lesser standard than strict scrutiny) was appropriate for measures that had been passed by Congress.

The Civil Rights Act of 1991

Metro Broadcasting had been a victory for affirmative action. But many of its supporters still felt threatened by the *Wards Cove* ruling. They felt it left companies with little reason to diversify their workforce. In 1991, they pushed another Civil Rights Act through Congress. Its twofold purpose was to:

> (1) respond to the Supreme Court's recent decisions by restoring the civil rights protections that were dramatically limited by those decisions; and

> (2) strengthen existing protections and remedies available under Federal civil rights laws to provide more effective deterrence and adequate compensation for victims of discrimination.[15]

Simply put, this meant that employers could not get away with discrimination. If they were found guilty of unfairly treating minorities, they were subject to penalties. The new law overrode parts of the *Wards Cove* decision. The burden of proof in discrimination cases was put once more on the employers instead of the workers. Companies had to prove that they were not discriminating.[16]

Strict Scrutiny Again: *Adarand Constructors, Inc.* v. *Pena*

What did all this mean for affirmative action? Did the *Metro Broadcasting* ruling mean the Supreme Court was backing down from the strict scrutiny test it had previously decreed? A lower standard—intermediate scrutiny—would allow more affirmative action programs to succeed. Naturally, white-owned companies that lost work to minorities disagreed with the more relaxed standard. One of these was Adarand Construction Company in Colorado. The owner, Randy Pech, hoped to receive a contract to build a guardrail in the San Juan National Forest. But although he submitted the lowest bid, the job went to a Hispanic-owned company. Pech believed he had lost the contract because he was white. He sued Federico Pena, the secretary of transportation, who was responsible for the contracts.

By the time *Adarand Constructors* v. *Pena* reached the Supreme Court, two justices had retired, including Thurgood Marshall. He was replaced by Clarence Thomas, an African American whose views differed greatly from those of his predecessor. Earlier, Thomas had said: "Government-sponsored racial discrimination based on benign [good] prejudice" was just as wrong as "discrimination inspired by malicious [evil] prejudice."[17] In other words, prejudice was prejudice, whether it singled out a group of people to help them or to harm them.

In a 5–4 decision, Justice Thomas's vote was crucial in overturning the two lower courts and in upholding the standard of strict scrutiny for all federal affirmative action programs.[18] This reversed the Supreme Court's earlier ruling in the *Metro Broadcasting* case. Affirmative action programs had to be limited to very specific situations such as a particular company or school that discriminated. Programs could not attempt to deal with the broader discrimination that existed throughout society.

Justice Scalia wanted to go even further. He doubted that there could ever be a "compelling interest" strong enough to justify the use of racial preferences. "Under our Constitution, there can be no such thing as either a creditor or a debtor race," Scalia said. "In the eyes of the government, we are just one race here. It is American."[19]

Scalia was not alone in thinking it was time for racial preferences to end. But plenty of people stood ready to oppose him. Even the president of the United States felt it was time to clarify and champion affirmative action.

chapter 8

Ongoing Debate

On July 19, 1995, less than a month after the *Adarand* decision, President Bill Clinton made an important speech on affirmative action. He spoke of the segregation and discrimination that he witnessed growing up in Arkansas in the 1950s and 1960s. In response to those who claimed that affirmative action was no longer needed, the president pointed out that African Americans were twice as likely to be out of work as whites. The unemployment rate for Hispanics was even worse. According to the Glass Ceiling Report, which had been commissioned by members of Congress, white males held 95 percent of the senior management positions in large corporations, even though they made up only 43 percent of the workforce.[1]

Mend It, Don't End It

President Clinton believed that all affirmative action programs should be guided by four principles: (1) no strict quotas; (2) no reverse discrimination; (3) no selection of unqualified individuals; and (4) no continuation of a program once its goal is achieved.[2] "But let me be clear," the president declared:

> Affirmative action has been good for America. . . .
> The job of ending discrimination in this country is not over. . . . So here is what I think we should do. We should reaffirm the principle of affirmative action and fix the practices. We should have a simple slogan: Mend it, but don't end it.[3]

Ward Connerly's Campaign

The day after Clinton's speech, however, the governing board, or regents, of the University of California had to face just that decision—whether to end affirmative action. Ward Connerly introduced two resolutions that would ban racial preferences in faculty hiring and in student admissions. Calling for better grade school and high school education, Connerly called affirmative action "a microscopic Band-Aid" on the problem of minority underachievement.[4]

The meeting room was packed as the regents prepared to vote on Connerly's controversial proposals. Despite forceful opposition, including a passionate speech from Reverend Jesse Jackson, the resolutions passed.

Shortly after this victory, Connerly was asked to become chairman of an anti–affirmative action group called the California Civil Rights Initiative. Two educators, Tom Wood and Glynn Custred, had prepared a measure that called for the elimination of affirmative action throughout the state. Under Connerly's leadership, the initiative received over a million signatures and qualified to go on the ballot for the 1997 election. Officially termed Proposition 209, the measure succeeded. Racial preferences became illegal in "public employment, public education, or public contracting."[5] Not only was the university forbidden to practice affirmative action, so were government agencies. There were to be absolutely no set-asides for minorities.

Many people viewed this situation with dismay. But Connerly called the passage of Proposition 209 "a victory for all of us."[6] In his election-night speech, he confidently declared, "We ended the illusion that our government can give some of us a preference based on skin color or gender and have that practice be regarded as something other than discrimination."[7]

More Bans on Affirmative Action

In 1998, voters in Washington State followed California's lead and passed Initiative 200, which also enforced a state-wide ban on affirmative action. One year later, Governor Jeb Bush issued an executive order that ended racial preferences in Florida's state universities. In place of affirmative action, he substituted the Talented 20 Program, a plan similar to the one begun in Texas after the *Hopwood* case. The top 20 percent of students graduating from their high schools would be guaranteed admission into one of Florida's state universities.[8]

California Governor Gray Davis also wanted to assure outstanding high school seniors of acceptance at the University of California. Under his direction, the top 4 percent of each high school graduating class was admitted to one of the university's eight campuses.[9]

Do percent plans work? Are they enough, by themselves, to ensure diversity in public schools? According to reports issued by the Harvard Civil Rights Project, enrollment in the public universities does not reflect the rapid growth of minority populations in California, Florida, and Texas.[10] In the very top schools, the number of minority students tends to be even lower. Patricia Marin, a Harvard researcher who worked on the reports, does not believe percent plans "offer a good alternative to race-conscious admissions programs." She has even called too great a reliance on them "dangerous."[11]

Focus of the Nation

The effectiveness of percent programs took on even more urgency as the Supreme Court prepared to hear two new cases in 2003. Jennifer Gratz, an outstanding high school student who was white, had been rejected by the University of Michigan at Ann Arbor in 1995. In the point system used by the university to evaluate students, extra points were automatically awarded to minority applicants. "I believe I was racially discriminated against, and that's wrong," Gratz said.[12]

Barbara Grutter, also white, was a forty-three-year-old business consultant who was rejected by the law school at the University of Michigan. She too was disturbed by the school's affirmative action program. Although the law school did not give extra points to minority applicants, it did make race a factor in the selection process. This seemed unfair to Grutter. Upon investigation, she learned that African Americans and other minorities with lower test scores than her own had been admitted to the university.

Both cases cited Lee Bollinger, the university's president, as the first defendant. "The primary reason for this [admissions procedure] was educational," Bollinger said, "a belief that . . . students . . . needed to be in an environment that reflected to some extent the diversity of American society."[13]

Terence Pell of the Center for Individual Rights, which helped both Gratz and Grutter file their lawsuits, disagreed. "You may not take race into account if the sole purpose is to achieve some bureaucrat's idea of the proper racial mix of the entering class. That is unconstitutional."[14]

The Lower Courts Rule

By the time *Gratz* v. *Bollinger* came to the federal district court in Detroit, the university had changed the way it reviewed undergraduate applications. Although minority students still received extra points, the court ruled that the changes made a big difference. The new admissions procedures were upheld, but the old ones were held to be unconstitutional.[15] Gratz, however, felt that even the new policy gave an unfair advantage to minorities. In a way, both Gratz and the university had won.

By contrast, the victory in *Grutter* v. *Bollinger* belonged entirely to Barbara Grutter and those who had filed suit with her. The court found the admissions system in the law school to be "practically indistinguishable from a quota" and a violation of the Equal Protection Clause of the Fourteenth Amendment.[16]

Although both cases went on to the U.S. Court of Appeals for the Sixth Circuit, a ruling was never made in the *Gratz* case. However, the appeals court overturned the lower court ruling in the *Grutter* case. In a 5–4 decision, the court said that diversity was a compelling state interest.[17] The law school had a right to take race into consideration when admitting students.

Gratz and *Grutter* were argued before the Supreme Court on the same day. Thousands of people marched outside the building as oral arguments were heard. Most were demonstrating in favor of affirmative action. Dozens of major companies throughout the nation were also supporting the policies of the University of Michigan. On the other side, the Bush administration supported Jennifer Gratz and Barbara Grutter in their quest to get the affirmative action policies overturned.

The Court had made many decisions on racial preferences in the workplace. But this would be the first Supreme Court ruling on affirmative action in higher education since the *Bakke* case twenty-five years earlier. It had the potential to revolutionize the way colleges selected students.

Gratz v. Bollinger

On June 23, 2003, the Supreme Court handed down both rulings. Once again, the Court was divided. Six of the nine justices ruled that the point system used to select students at the University of Michigan violated the Equal Protection Clause of the Fourteenth Amendment. The automatic advantage it gave to minorities was too rigid. Because it was not narrowly tailored enough, it did more than was strictly necessary to achieve racial and ethnic diversity on campus. For these reasons, the lower court ruling was overturned and the undergraduate affirmative action program was struck down.[18]

Jennifer Gratz cried when she heard the ruling announced on television. By then she had graduated from the University of Michigan at Dearborn and was working for a software company in San Diego. "Some [tears] were tears of happiness," she said. "I am glad I took a stand for what I believe in. I will continue to stand up for what I believe in . . . forever."[19]

Grutter v. Bollinger

The justices felt differently when it came to the law school's admission program. In a 5–4 decision, the Court agreed with the lower court's ruling and upheld the law school's affirmative action policy. Sandra Day O'Connor, who wrote the majority opinion, noted that diversity among the student body is "a compelling state interest that can justify the use of race in university admissions."[20] She also noted that although school officials made race a "plus" factor, it was not the deciding factor in the

Barbara Grutter (left) and Jennifer Gratz sued the University of Michigan in cases that reached the Supreme Court in 2003. The Court ruled that the rigid point system used to exclude Gratz was unconstitutional, but it upheld the affirmative action policy of the law school, which had not admitted Grutter.

admissions process. Looking to the future, O'Connor wrote, "We expect that 25 years from now, the use of racial preferences will no longer be necessary to further the interest approved today."[21]

Although Gratz is important, Grutter may ultimately prove the more significant decision. This ruling, based on Justice Powell's reasoning, both supports and limits affirmative action. It leaves plenty of room for discussion.

The Legacy of the *Taxman* Settlement

Almost six years had passed since the Black Leadership Forum had helped to keep Sharon Taxman's lawsuit against the Piscataway School District from reaching the Supreme Court in 1997. Some supporters of affirmative action felt that the *Taxman* settlement had made the favorable *Gratz* ruling possible. By preventing a decision in 1989 that might have shut down affirmative action programs across the country, the Black Leadership Forum had allowed public discussions and Congressional investigations to continue. In other words, they had kept the affirmative action debate alive.[22]

Turnabout in Texas

The Supreme Court's acceptance of affirmative action in the *Grutter* case had the biggest impact in Texas, Louisiana, and Mississippi. Seven years earlier, the Fifth Circuit Appeals Court had struck down affirmative action in *Hopwood* v. *Texas*. But the new Supreme Court ruling overrode the earlier decision. Public universities in these states were free to use affirmative action again. Almost immediately, Dr. Larry R. Faulkner, president of the University of Texas at Austin, held a news conference. "We need to fairly quickly modify our admissions procedures to take race into account," he said.[23] This would make an especially big difference in graduate programs and law and medical schools, which had never been covered by the Texas Ten Percent Plan.

"There is a compelling responsibility," said Faulkner, "for a central public institution like this one to act directly and positively to educate the leadership of the future. That leadership comes from all sectors of society. . . . Today's court decision makes it easier for us to accomplish that goal."[24]

Continuing Controversy

The arguments on racial preferences are far from over. While *Grutter* v. *Bollinger* was good news for affirmative action policies, *Gratz* v. *Bollinger* put strict limits on those policies. Soon after the cases were decided, Grutter and Gratz joined the Michigan Civil Rights Initiative Committee, which seeks to ban affirmative action by popular vote as California did. "People need to remember that the Court doesn't have the last word here," said Barbara Grutter when the initiative was announced. "It remains open for the people of each state to end race preferences because they are morally wrong and harmful to both individuals and society."[25]

Meanwhile, a national organization named By Any Means Necessary is fighting to overthrow

Proposition 209 and make affirmative action legal once more in California. "Race-conscious measures are still necessary to achieve what *Brown* prescribed as the only road to equality," asserts Luke Massie, codirector of the group.[26]

More questions and challenges are bound to arise as new affirmative action programs are developed. But whatever one's views on racial preferences, most people share the same goal—an open society in which all races and ethnic groups enjoy the same opportunity for happiness and success. They simply disagree on how to get there.

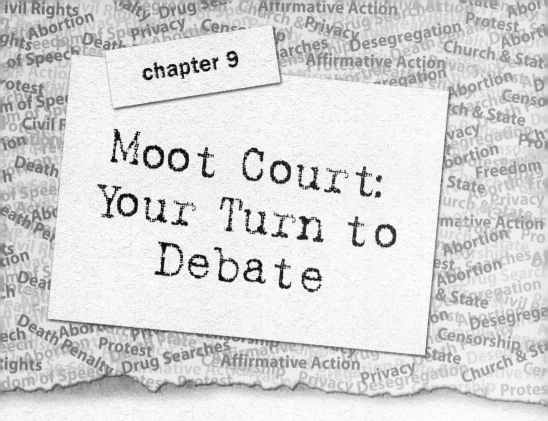

Moot Court: Your Turn to Debate

In this chapter, you will learn how to participate in a mock judicial proceeding of your own.[1] One type of court exercise is called "moot court." Moot court is a dramatization of a hypothetical (fictitious) or real case that went before an appeals court or the Supreme Court. The purpose of these courts is to rule on a lower court's decision. It is different from a trial in that no witnesses appear and testify, just as no witnesses are called in a Supreme Court case. Also, the focus is on whether the court below made any mistakes rather than on finding all the facts of a case.

In moot court, the players take the roles of judges, clerks, attorneys, and journalists. They do research, write briefs, and argue legal issues before a make-believe panel of appeals court judges. The exercise hones research, writing, and debate skills.

Taking part in a moot court is a fun way to get a feeling for how a real court case occurs. Try a moot activity with your class or club. Here's how.

Step 1: Assign Roles

Here are the roles you will need to fill:

◇ Judges. If the group is large enough, have nine justices like the Supreme Court has. Otherwise, have a panel of three appellate court judges. Choose one person to be Chief Justice and direct the proceeding. The judges hear the attorney's arguments, question them, and then write and deliver the final ruling. The court's majority opinion is the position agreed upon by a majority of the panel. Individual judges may choose to issue concurring or dissenting opinions of their own.

◇ Two or more court clerks. They work with the judges to prepare five or more questions to ask the attorneys during oral arguments. Judicial clerks also help with the research for judges' opinions.

◇ A team of two or more attorneys for the appellant. They feel the lower court was wrong.

◇ A team of two or more attorneys for the appellee. They believe the lower court ruled correctly.

◇ A designated spokesperson to present the argument (though any of the attorneys can answer questions from the judges). Attorneys must address the major issues by presenting the most persuasive arguments for their side.

◇ Two or more reporters. They interview the attorneys before the case and write news stories about the facts of the case and the final ruling.

◇ The bailiff, who calls the court to order. The bailiff will also time each side's oral argument.

Step 2: Prepare Your Case: *Amy Anderson* v. *University of the Western Plains*

Part 1: Gather Information

The case you will hear and decide is based on *Gratz v. Bollinger*.

The situation:

(1) The Appellant's View

The appellant, Amy Anderson, has worked hard throughout her four years of high school. She has excellent grades and test scores. Neither of her parents has attended college, and they cannot afford to send her to an expensive school. Amy decides to attend a large and well-respected state university. Her academic record is so strong that she feels certain of acceptance. She does not apply to any other college.

To Amy's surprise and disappointment, she is not accepted at the university after all. She has to change her plans and make an application to a less selective college. Later, however, she learns that the affirmative action program of her first-choice school allowed minority students to gain admittance who did not have her high grades or test scores. She feels very strongly that this is unfair. After talking with several people from a law center, she begins to think that the university's actions were illegal. She has been discriminated against because she is white, and that is forbidden by the Constitution. Amy seeks out other qualified individuals who have been rejected by the university. They decide to join her in a lawsuit. She names the president of the university as well as other school officials in the suit.

(2) The Appellee's View

The university president, Dr. Wayne Miller, the appellee, feels equally strongly about his position. He considers it a matter of the utmost importance to have a student body that reflects the racial and ethnic diversity in society. This is for the good of all the students—not just minorities. Diversity on campus leads to an exchange of ideas, viewpoints, and culture that enrich the educational experience. It also promotes tolerance and understanding. The president and the other officials do not believe that there is anything in the Constitution to keep them from setting an admissions policy for the good of the University of the Western Plains.

Dr. Miller further believes that the university's affirmative action policy conforms to the guidelines specified by the Supreme Court in *Regents of the University of California* v. *Bakke*. There are no quotas. Race is only one of several factors the university takes into consideration when admitting students. Some of the others include grades, test scores, recommendations, activities, and overcoming challenges. Although race is never the deciding factor, when everything else is equal, it is a definite plus. The university also has special scholarships and outreach programs for minorities that are not available to white applicants.

The minority students who are admitted under the affirmative action program may not have the highest test scores, but they have worked hard and are eager to do well. Many (but not all) of them come from families that could not give them extra advantages such as music or art lessons or summer camp. Their parents have been completely focused on providing the basics. Although these students may not be the best qualified in terms of strict academics, they are smart, highly motivated, and capable of doing the course work they will encounter. Their knowledge and success will become an inspiration to others in their communities. The university believes that it can give these students a good education, and that they, in turn, can add an important dimension to campus life.

Amy's case goes all the way to the Supreme Court. The two sides are made up of the following people:

◇ Amy (the appellant), several other students in her position who have decided to join the lawsuit, and the appellant's lawyers. They must prove that the university's affirmative action policy violates the Equal Protection Clause of the Fourteenth Amendment and the Civil Rights Act of 1964. They take the position that discrimination is equally wrong whether it is suffered by blacks or whites.

◇ The university president, Dr. Miller (the appellee), other school officials who are responsible for the admissions policy, and the appellee's lawyers. According to recent Supreme Court rulings, the appellee's lawyers must prove first that diversity on campus is a "compelling state interest," that it is of vital importance to the students who attend the university. Second, they must prove that the affirmative action policy is "narrowly tailored" to achieve this important goal. It must not be seen as a means to atone for past injustice in society or to remedy discrimination that exists beyond the university.

Part 2: Write Your Briefs

A legal brief is a written presentation of your argument. Brainstorm with the lawyers on your team. Which arguments are strongest for you? What are your weaknesses?

You may want to divide up arguments for research and writing. If so, be sure to work as a team to put the brief together. Otherwise, your brief may have holes or read poorly.

Use the arguments above as suggestions, and think of arguments of your own that might sway the opinion of the court in your favor. Each legal team should also look to past Supreme Court decisions (as presented in this book). Establishing legal precedent (showing how the outcome they want follows logically from past decisions) helps to strengthen the case. The lawyers should also discuss what a decision for or against them would mean to society.

In real life, court rules spell out what briefs must contain. Use these rules for your moot court activity.

1. The cover page should have the case name, *Amy Anderson* v. *University of the Western Plains*, and say whether it is the case for the appellant or the appellee. List the lawyers' names.

2. The text of the brief should have these sections:

   A. Statement of the issue for review: What question is before the court?

   B. Statement of the case: What is this case about? How did the trial court rule?

   C. Statement of the facts: Briefly describe the facts relevant to the case.

   D. Summary of the arguments: Sum up your argument in 150 words or less.

   E. Argument: Spell out the legal arguments that support your side. You can split this into sections with subheadings for each part. Include references to cases or authorities that help your side.

   F. Conclusion: Ask the court to rule for your client.

3. Real appeals briefs may be thirty pages long. Limit your brief to no more than five typed pages, double spaced, or about 1,250 words. If possible, type on a computer. Otherwise, write very neatly.

4. On an agreed-upon date, each team gives the other a copy of its brief. Each judge gets a copy too. If you do this in class, give the teacher a copy. Be sure each team member keeps a copy of the brief too.

In real life, lawyers often prepare reply briefs. They must answer points made by the other side.

You will not do that. But you should be ready to answer their points in oral argument.

Part 3: Prepare for Oral Argument
Each side will have up to fifteen minutes to argue its case. One or two students from each side should be chosen to present the strongest arguments to the judges. They should practice their speeches so they can get through the most important arguments in the set amount of time.

While the lawyers are putting together their arguments, the journalists quietly visit both groups and take notes on what is happening. They write the lead paragraph of newspaper story about the case, explaining the major issues and the impact the decision is expected to have. These can be posted on the bulletin board.

The judges are also going over the facts. Judges should read all the briefs before oral arguments. Their discussion may include reviewing past cases and deciding what questions they would like to ask each set of lawyers. The clerks review the case with the judges and may suggest questions.

Step 3: Hold the Oral Argument
Part 1: Assemble the Participants

⬦ The judges sit in a panel at the head of the room. This is called the bench. They should not enter until the bailiff calls the court to order. A speaking podium faces the bench.

◇ The appellant's (Amy's) team of attorneys sits at one side, facing the judges.

◇ The appellee's (the university's) team sits at the opposite side, also facing the judges.

◇ The reporters sit at the back.

◇ As the judges enter, the bailiff calls the court to order: "Oyez (oy-yay)! Oyez! Oyez! The _____ Court of the United States is now in session with the Honorable Chief Justice _____ presiding. All will stand and remain standing until the judges are seated and the Chief Justice has asked all present to be seated."

Part 2: Present the Case

◇ The Chief Justice calls the case and asks whether the parties are ready. Each team's spokesperson answers "Yes."

◇ The appellant's spokesperson approaches the podium saying, "May it please the court." Then the argument begins. Judges interrupt when they wish to ask a question. The attorneys respectfully answer any questions as asked. Do not get flustered if a judge interrupts with a question. Answer the question honestly. Then move on.

◇ Then the appellee's team takes its turn.

◇ Each side has up to fifteen minutes to present its arguments. If the appellant's team wishes, it can save five minutes of its time to rebut the appellee's argument. If so, the spokesperson should inform the court before sitting down.

◇ After the arguments, the bailiff has everyone rise as the judges retire to chambers to debate their decision.

◇ At this time, reporters may interview lawyers for the parties and begin working on their articles.

◇ After an agreed-upon time, the judges return, and the Chief Justice announces the ruling that will determine Amy's future and affect affirmative action programs in schools across the nation.

Step 4: Publish and Report the Decision

A few days later, the court issues its majority opinion in written form, along with any dissenting opinions and individual concurring opinions. At the same time, the reporters' stories are made available.

With the announcement of the ruling, your mock trial is complete. In real life, the ruling marks both the end and the beginning. The courtroom procedures are over, but the work of implementing the decision can take months or years.

Questions for Discussion

1. Do you think that the striking differences in employment rates between blacks and whites indicate that discrimination still exists, or is there another explanation?

2. Is diversity in colleges and in the workplace a compelling state interest—that is, is it important enough to justify affirmative action programs?

3. What about Americans who are not members of minority groups? Are racial preferences fair to them?

4. Do you feel that affirmative action should be accepted as a means of remedying past discrimination?

5. Do you agree with Justice Blackmun when he says that you have to use race in order to get beyond race?

6. Should there be affirmative action programs for Americans, regardless of race, who have low incomes?

7. What is the difference between strong affirmative action and weak affirmative action?

8. Are there ways in which affirmative action benefits everyone—not just members of minority groups?

9. What is the difference between strict scrutiny and intermediate scrutiny? Which standard do you think should be used to judge affirmative action programs?

10. Is affirmative action demeaning to minorities?

11. Sandra Day O'Connor has said she does not expect affirmative action to be needed in twenty-five years. Do you agree with her? Why or why not?

12. Do you think that affirmative action programs violate the Constitution? Or do you think it is permissible to take race into consideration as long as there is no intent to insult or harm anyone?

Chapter Notes

Chapter 1. A Tale of Two Teachers

1. Mark Walsh, "Layoff Case Is Personal In N.J. School," *Education Week on the Web*, p. 5, October 8, 1997, <http://www.edweek.org/ew/vol-17/06piscat.h17> (January 31, 2004).

2. Ibid., p. 1.

3. Ibid., p. 4.

4. John W. Alexander, "Affirmative action case atop '97–'98 high-court agenda," *World Magazine*, vol. 12, no. 20, October 4, 1997, <http://www.worldmag.com/world/issue/10-04-97/national__2.asp>

5. Walsh, p. 2.

6. Nat Hentoff, "Sacrificed to Affirmative Action," *The Washington Post*, p. A23, November 29, 1997, <http://www.washingtonpost.com/wpsrv/politics/special/affirm/stories/aaop112997.htm> (September 13, 2003).

7. Ibid.

8. Ibid.

9. Linda Greenhouse, "Settlement Ends High Court Case On Preferences: Tactical Retreat," *New York Times*, November 22, 1997, <http://www.pulitzer.org/year/1998/beat-reporting/works/> (March 22, 2005).

10. Yvonne Scruggs-Leftwich, "Understanding the Piscataway Settlement," *Publications & Speeches: Black Leadership Forum, Inc.*, copyright 2002–2003, <http://www.blackleadershipforum.org/articles/piscataway.html> (April, 29, 2005).

Chapter 2. A Long, Unequal Struggle

1. Stephan Thernstrom and Abigail Thernstrom, *America in Black and White: One Nation, Indivisible* (New York: Simon & Schuster, 1997), pp. 30–31.

2. *Freedom: A History of Us*, Webisode 7, segment 7, "Separate but Equal," <http://www.pbs.org/wnet/historyofus/web07/segment7.html> (March 22, 2005).

3. *Plessy* v. *Ferguson*. 163 U.S. 537; 16 S. Ct. 1138; 41 L. ed. 256 (1896).

4. Ibid.

5. Thernstrom and Thernstrom, p. 37.

6. Ibid., p. 36.

7. James Oliver Horton and Lois E. Horton, *Hard Road to Freedom: The Story of African America* (New Brunswick, N.J., and London: Rutgers University Press, 2001), p. 269.

8. Charles J. Ogletree, Jr., *All Deliberate Speed: Reflections on the First Half Century of* Brown v. Board of Education (New York and London: W. W. Norton & Company, 2004), p. 121.

9. *Sweatt* v. *Painter*. 126th District Court of Travis County, Texas, N. 74, 945.

10. *U.S. Law Week*, vol. 18, April 11, 1950, <http://www.law.du.edu/russell/in/Sweatt/US/w41150.html> (May 11, 2005).

11. Juan Williams, *Eyes on the Prize: America's Civil Rights Years, 1954–1965* (New York: Penguin Books, 1988), pp. 16–17.

12. *Sweatt* v. *Painter* et al. 339 U.S. 629; 70 S. Ct. 848; 94 L. Ed. 1114 (1950).

13. *McLaurin* v. *Oklahoma State Regents*. 339 U.S. 637 (1950).

14. Williams, p. 18.

15. Cheryl Brown Henderson, "Personal Perspective: *Brown* v. *Board* 50th Anniversary," *The Brown Quarterly*, vol. 5, no. 3, Winter 2003, <http://brownvboard.org/brwnqurt/05-3/05-3b.htm> (January 1, 2005).

16. Williams, p. 20.

17. Williams, p. 19.

18. Ogletree, p. 124.

19. *Brown et al.* v. *Board of Education of Topeka, Shawnee County, Kansas, et al.; Briggs et al.* v. *Elliott et al.; Davis et al.* v. *County School Board of Prince Edward County, VA et al.; Gebhart et al.* v. *Belton et al.* 347 U.S. 483; 74 S. Ct. 686; 98 L. Ed. 873 (1954).

20. Henderson.

21. Jane S. Smith, *Patenting the Sun: Polio and the Salk Vaccine* (New York: William Morrow, 1990), p. 273.

22. *Brown* v. *Board of Education.* 349 U.S. 294 (1955).

23. "The Southern Manifesto," 102 Cong. Rec. 4515-16 (1956), <http://www.eviog.uga.edu/Projects/gainfo/manifesto.htm> (May 11, 2005).

24. Ogletree, p. 126.

25. Thernstrom, p. 106.

26. Williams, p. 107.

27. Ogletree, p. 128.

28. *Green* v. *County School Board.* 391 U.S. 430 (1968).

29. Ibid.

30. Thernstrom and Thernstrom, pp. 105 and 317.

Chapter 3. Freedom Is Not Enough: The Rise of Affirmative Action

1. Juan Williams, *Eyes on the Prize: America's Civil Rights Years, 1954–1965* (New York: Penguin Books, 1988), p. 74.

2. Stephan Thernstrom and Abigail Thernstrom, *America in Black and White: One Nation, Indivisible* (New York: Simon and Schuster, 1997), p. 109. Quoted from Martin Luther King, Jr., *Stride Toward Freedom: The Montgomery Story* (New York: Harper & Row, 1958), pp. 126–130.

3. Thernstrom and Thernstrom, p. 123.

4. Executive Order No. 10925. 26 FR 1977, 1961 WL 8178 (Pres.).

5. Carl Cohen and James P. Sterba, *Affirmative Action and Racial Preference: A Debate* (Oxford and New York: Oxford University Press, 2003), p. 191.

6. John F. Kennedy, "Radio and Television Report to the American People on Civil Rights," The White House, *John F. Kennedy Library and Museum*, June 11, 1963, <http://www.cs.umb.edu.jfklibrary/j061163.htm> (March 25, 2004).

7. Thernstrom and Thernstrom, p. 150.

8. James Oliver Horton and Lois E. Horton, *Hard Road to Freedom: The Story of African America* (New Brunswick, N.J., and London: Rutgers University Press, 2001), p. 298.

9. President Lyndon B. Johnson's Commencement Address at Howard University: "To Fulfill These Rights," *Lyndon Baines Johnson Library and Museum*, June 4, 1965, <http://www.lbjlib.utexas.edu/johnson/archives.hom/speeches.hom/650604.asp> (March 22, 2005).

10. Thernstrom and Thernstrom, p. 157.

11. Executive Order 11246, *Division of Human Resources Employment*, <http://www.hr.ucdavis.edu/Emp/SAAD/03_Policies_and_Laws/Executive_Order_11246> (March 25, 2004).

12. Nicholas Lemann, "Taking Affirmative Action Apart" in *Affirmative Action: Social Justice or Reverse Discrimination?* Francis J. Beckwith and Todd E. Jones, eds. (Amherst, New York: Prometheus Books, 1997), p. 42.

13. Borgna Brunner, Infoplease, "Timeline of Affirmative Action Milestones," 2000–2005, <http://www.infoplease.com/spot/affirmativetimeline1.html> (May 10, 2005).

14. Cohen and Sterba, p. 193.

15. Ibid.

16. Thomas Sowell, "From Equal Opportunity to 'Affirmative Action'" in *Affirmative Action: Social Justice or Reverse Discrimination?* Beckwith and Jones, eds., p. 102.

17. Lemann, p. 50.

18. Beckwith and Jones, eds., p. 11.

19. Ibid., p. 12.

Chapter 4. The Pros of Affirmative Action: Leveling the Playing Field

1. Francis J. Beckwith and Todd E. Jones, eds., *Affirmative Action: Social Justice or Reverse Discrimination?* (Amherst, N.Y.: Prometheus Books, 1997), p. 10.

2. Ibid.

3. Martin Garbus, *Courting Disaster: The Supreme Court and the Unmaking of American Law* (New York: Henry Holt and Company, 2002), p. 208.

4. Ibid.

5. Tom L. Beauchamp, "In Favor of Affirmative Action," in *The Affirmative Action Debate*, Steven M. Cahn, ed. (New York and London: Routledge, 2002), p. 211. Beauchamp's article reprinted from Journal of Ethics 2 (1998).

6. Colin L. Powell, Secretary of State, United States of America, interview, May 23, 1998, Jackson Hole, Wyoming, *Academy of Achievement: A Museum of Living History*, <http://www.achievement.org/autodoc/page/pow0int-1> (March 22, 2005).

7. "Powell defends affirmative action in college admissions," *CNN.com/Inside Politics*, January 20, 2003, <http://www.cnn.com/2003/ALLPOLITICS/01/19/powell.race/> (April 29, 2005).

8. Charles J. Ogletree, Jr., "The Case for Affirmative Action," *Stanford Magazine*, p. 1, 1996, <http://www.stanfordalumni.org/news/magazine/1996/sepoct/articles/for.html> (November 8, 2004).

9. Philip Rucker, "Broaden affirmative action, Simmons says," *Yaledailynews.com*, April 10, 2003, <http://yaledailynews.com/article.asp?AID=22512> (March 22, 2005).

10. Ibid.

11. W. Avon Drake and Robert D. Holsworth, *Affirmative Action and the Stalled Quest for Black Power* (Urbana and Chicago: University of Illinois Press, 1996), p. 14.

12. Ibid., p. 14.

13. Natasha Smith, "Affirmative Action May Join the Halls of History," *DistrictChronicles.com*, March 27, 2003, <http://www.districtchronicles.com/news/2003/03/27/Neighborhood/Affirmative.Action.May.Join.The.Halls.Of.History-400553.shtml> (January 3, 2005).

Chapter 5. The Cons of Affirmative Action: Reverse Discrimination

1. Carl Cohen and James P. Sterba, *Affirmative Action and Racial Preference: A Debate* (Oxford and New York: Oxford University Press, 2003), pp. 109, 121.

2. Stephan Thernstrom and Abigail Thernstrom, *America in Black and White: One Nation, Indivisible* (New York: Simon & Schuster, 1997), pp. 405–406.

3. Ibid.

4. Ibid.

5. Dinesh D'Souza, *The End of Racism* (New York: The Free Press, 1995), p. 289.

6. Thomas Sowell, "From Equal Opportunity to 'Affirmative Action,'" in *Affirmative Action: Social Justice or Reverse Discrimination?* Francis J. Beckwith and Todd E. Jones, eds. (Amherst, N.Y.: Prometheus Books, 1997), p. 110.

7. Cohen and Sterba, p. 27.

8. Ibid., p. 117.

9. Ward Connerly, *Creating Equal: My Fight Against Race Preferences* (San Francisco: Encounter Books, 2000), p. 116.

10. "Ward Connerly: A Black Man Leads the Fight Against Anti-White Bias," *NewsMax.Com Wires* and *NewsMax.Com*, May 5, 2003, <http://www.newsmax.com/archives/articles/2003/5/5/151446.shtml> (January 4, 2005).

Chapter 6. Challenges in Education

1. Howard Ball, *The Bakke Case: Race, Education, and Affirmative Action* (Lawrence: University Press of Kansas, 2000), p. 47.

2. Ibid., p. 77.

3. Ibid., p. 88.

4. Martin Garbus, *Courting Disaster: The Supreme Court and the Unmaking of American Law* (New York: Henry Holt and Company, 2002), p. 230.

5. Ball, p. 95.

6. Ibid., p. 96.

7. *deFunis* v. *Odegaard*, 416 U.S. 312 (1974).

8. Kermit L. Hall, ed., *The Oxford Guide to United States Supreme Court Decisions* (Oxford and New York: Oxford University Press, 1999), p. 253.

9. Ibid.

10. *Regents of the University of California v. Bakke*, 438 U.S. 265; 98 S. Ct. 2733; 57 L. Ed. 2d 750 (1978).

11. Hall, p. 253.

12. Ball, p. 124.

13. Garbus, p. 230.

14. *Regents of the University of California v. Bakke*.

15. *Wygant et al. v. Jackson Board of Education et al.* 476 U.S. 267; 106 S. Ct. 1842; 90 L. Ed. 2d 260 (1986).

16. Ibid.

17. Cheryl J. Hopwood, et al., Plaintiffs-Appelees, versus state of Texas, et al., Defendants, Appellees. No. 94–50569, No. 94–50664; United States Court of Appeals for the Fifth Circuit, 78 F3d 932; 1996 U.S. App. LEXIS 4719, March 1996, Decided.

18. Henry J. Reske, "Law school affirmative action in doubt: 5th Circuit ruling strikes down University of Texas admission preferences," *The ABA Journal*, May 11, 1996, <http://www.cir-usa.org/articles/36.html> (January 5, 2005).

19. Rose Gutfeld, "Ten Percent in Texas: The jury is still out on an alternative to affirmative action," *Ford Foundation Report*, Fall 2002, <http://www.fordfound.org/publications/ff_report/view_ss_report_detail.cfm?report_index=355> (January 5, 2005).

20. Brian Henn, "Sociology professor finds 10 percent plan flawed," *DailyPrincetonian.com*, February 4, 2003, <http://

www.dailyprincetonian.com/archives/2003/02/04/news/
7170.shtml> (January 5, 2005).

21. Gutfeld.

22. Frances Carroll, "Donation helps end teacher's bias case," *Home News Tribune*, November 22, 1997.

23. Ibid.

24. Frances Carroll, "Fear of verdict's impact fueled settlement," *Home News Tribune*, November 22, 1997.

25. Ibid.

Chapter 7. Challenges in the Workplace

1. *Griggs et al.* v. *Duke Power Co.*, 401 U .S. 424; 91 S. Ct. 849; 28 L. Ed. 2d 158 (1971).

2. Stephan Thernstrom and Abigail Thernstrom, *America in Black and White: One Nation, Indivisible* (New York: Simon & Schuster, 1997), pp. 433–434.

3. *United Steelworkers* v. *Weber*, 443 U.S. 193; 99 S. Ct. 2721; 61 L. ed. 2d 480 (1979).

4. *Fullilove et al.* v. *Klutznick, Secretary of Commerce, et al.* 488 U.S. 448; 100 S. Ct. 2758; 65 L. Ed. 2d 902 (1980).

5. Thernstrom and Thernstrom, pp. 435–436.

6. *Johnson* v. *Transportation Agency.* 480 U.S. 616 (1987).

7. W. Avon Drake and Roger D. Holsworth, *Affirmative Action and the Stalled Quest for Black Progress* (Urbana and Chicago: University of Illinois Press, 1996), p. 81.

8. Ibid.

9. *City of Richmond, Appellant* v. *J.A. Croson Company*; 488 U .S. 469; 109 S. Ct. 706; 102 L. Ed. 2d 854 (1989).

10. Thernstrom and Thernstrom, p. 437.

11. *City of Richmond, Appellant* v. *J.A. Croson Company*; 488 U .S. 469; 109 S. Ct. 706; 102 L. Ed. 2d 854 (1989).

12. Thernstrom and Thernstrom, p. 438.

13. Ibid.; Kermit L. Hall, ed., *The Oxford Guide to United States Supreme Court Decisions* (Oxford and New York: Oxford University Press, 1999), p. 115.

14. *Metro Broadcasting, Inc.* v. *FCC*, 497 U.S. 547; 110 S. Ct. 2997; 111 L. Ed. 2d 445 (1990).

15. Civil Rights Act of 1991, 102d Congress, 1st session, <http://usinfo.state.gov/usa/infousa/laws/majorlaw/civil91.htm> (March 22, 2005).

16. Thernstrom and Thernstrom, p. 439.

17. Martin Garbus, *Courting Disaster: The Supreme Court and the Unmaking of American Law* (New York: Henry Holt and Company, 2002), p. 240.

18. Thernstrom and Thernstrom, p. 454.

19. *Adarand Constructors, Inc., Petitioner* v. *Federica Pena, Secretary of Transportation et al.* 515 U.S. 200; 115 S. Ct. 2097; 132 L. Ed. 2d 158 (1995).

Chapter 8. Ongoing Debate

1. "The Job of Ending Discrimination in This Country Is Not Over," *washingtonpost.com*, July 19, 1995, <http://www.washingtonpost.com/wp-srv/politics/special/affirm/docs/clintonspeech.htm> (March 22, 2005).

2. Ibid.

3. Ibid.

4. Ward Connerly, *Creating Equal: My Fight Against Race Preferences* (San Francisco: Encounter Books, 2000), p. 145.

5. "Proposition 209: Text of Proposed Law," *CA Secretary of State—Vote 96,* <http://vote96.ss.ca.gov/vote96/html/BP/209text.htm> (July 4, 2004).

6. Ward Connerly, "The Sweet Music of Equal Treatment," in *Affirmative Action: Social Justice or Reverse Discrimination?* Francis J. Beckwith and Todd E. Jones, eds. (Amherst, N.Y.: Prometheus Books, 1997), p. 64.

7. Ibid., p. 65.

8. "Percent Plans: How Successful Are They?" *Diversity Digest*, vol. 7, *DiversityWeb: An Interactive Resource Hub for Higher Education*, July 2003, <http://www.diversityweb.org/digest/vol7no1-2/percent_plans.cfm> (July 4, 2004).

9. Ibid.

10. Catherine L. Horn and Stella M. Flores, foreword by Gary Orfield, "Percent Plans in College Admissions: A Comparative Analysis of Three States' Experiences," *The Civil Rights Project: Harvard University*, February 7, 2003, <http://www.civilrightsproject.harvard.edu/research/affirmativeaction/tristate.php> (July 4, 2004).

11. Michael A. Fletcher, "College 'Percent' Plan May Not Help Diversity: Minority Enrollment Tends to Be Lower at Selective Schools, Report Finds," *washingtonpost.com*, February 11, 2003, <http://aad.english.ucsb.edu/docs/collegepercentplans20.html> (July 4, 2004).

12. "Testing the System," Newshour Transcript, reported by Elizabeth Brackett of WTTW Chicago, *Online NewsHour*, December 22, 1997, <http://www.pbs.org/newsHour/bb/education/july-dec97/michigan_12-22.html> (June 16, 2004).

13. Ibid.

14. Ibid.

15. Carl Cohen and James P. Sterba, *Affirmative Action and Racial Preference: A Debate* (Oxford: Oxford University Press, 2003), p. 183.

16. Ibid., p. 184.

17. Ibid., p. 185.

18. *Gratz* v. *Bollinger*, 539 U.S. 244; 123 S. Ct. 2411; 156 L.Ed. 2d 257 (2003).

19. Jodi S. Cohen, "Lead plaintiff celebrates: Southgate alum feels vindicated after beating U-M," *The Detroit News*, June 24, 2003, <http://www.detnews.com/2003/schools/0306/24/a08-201532.htm> (January 5, 2005).

20. *Grutter* v. *Bollinger*, 530 U.S. 306; 123 S. Ct. 2325; 156 L.Ed. 2d 304 (2003).

21. Ibid.

22. Yvonne Scruggs-Leftwich, "Affirmative Action Validated: Black Leaders' 1997 Boldness Made Possible Current Supreme Court Decision," *Black Leadership Forum*, June 24, 2003, <http://www.blackleadershipforum.org/articles/affirmaction2003.html> (July 4, 2004).

23. Jeffrey Selingo, "Ruling in the Affirmative," *AARP, Education Watch*, <http://www.aarp.org/nrta-watch/Articles/a2003-11-18-affirmative.html> (January 5, 2005).

24. News release, The University of Texas at Austin, "The University of Texas at Austin reacts to the Supreme Court's affirmative action decisions," June 23, 2003, <http://www.utexas.edu/opa/news/03newsreleases/nr200306/nraffirmativeaction030623.html> (January 5, 2005).

25. Barbara Grutter, plaintiff, *Grutter* v. *Bollinger*, Speeches, Announcement of the Michigan Civil Rights Initiative, July 8, 2003, <http://www.michigancivilrights.org/grutter/htm> (June 16, 2004).

26. Charles Proctor, "All sides of debate on Prop. 209 use ruling," *Daily Bruin, UCLA*, May 21, 2004, <http://www.dailybruin.ucla.edu/news/articles.asp?ID=29068> (June 13, 2004).

Chapter 9. Moot Court: Your Turn to Debate

1. The material in this chapter is adapted from Millie Aulbur, "Constitutional Issues and Teenagers," *The Missouri Bar*, n.d., <http://www.mobar.org/teach/clesson.htm> (December 10, 2004); Street Law, Inc., and The Supreme Court Historical Society, "Moot Court Activity," 2002, <http://www.landmarkcases.org> (December 10, 2004); with suggestions from Ron Fridell and Kathiann M. Kowalski.

Glossary

affirmative action—Policies or programs that give special advantages to minority groups in college admissions and in job hiring.

Civil Rights Act of 1964—Landmark legislation outlawing segregation in public and private facilities.

compelling state interest—Overwhelming government need to maintain or achieve a certain state of affairs, such as racial diversity in a school.

Equal Protection Clause—Portion of the Fourteenth Amendment to the Constitution that guarantees equal protection under the law to all citizens, regardless of race.

executive order—Presidential mandate to create or change public policy.

intermediate scrutiny—Moderate standard of evaluation used to judge the need for a policy such as affirmative action. Intermediate scrutiny requires strong reasons, but lawyers do not have to prove a compelling state interest.

narrowly defined—Term to describe a policy or plan that addresses a problem very specifically and does not overlap into other areas. It solves the problem and does nothing more.

percent plans—An alternative to race-conscious affirmative action in which a set percentage of top students from their high school graduating classes receive automatic entrance into certain state schools.

point system—An affirmative action policy that awards a set number of automatic points to college applicants who are members of minority groups.

quotas—A fixed number or fixed percentage of minority students who must be admitted to a college or a fixed number of minority job candidates who must be hired.

set-aside program—An affirmative action policy that reserves, or sets aside, a certain number of jobs for minority candidates or a certain percentage of business for minority companies.

strict scrutiny—An extremely demanding standard of evaluation. Two criteria must be met in order for a policy to pass strict scrutiny: (1) A compelling state interest must exist, and (2) the program must be narrowly tailored.

strong affirmative action—Affirmative action that involves setting racial goals or quotas.

weak affirmative action—Affirmative action that gives special favor to minority groups but does not set quotas.

Further Reading

Books

Beckman, James A. *Affirmative Action: An Encyclopedia*. Westport, Conn.: Greenwood Press, 2004.

Robinson, Jo Ann Ooiman, editor. *Affirmative Action: A Documentary History*. Westport, Conn.: Greenwood Press, 2001.

Stefoff, Rebecca. *The Bakke Case: Challenge to Affirmative Action*. New York: Marshall Cavendish Benchmark, 2005.

Williams, Mary E., editor. *Discrimination*. San Diego, Calif.: Greenhaven Press, 2003.

Internet Addresses

"Bakke and Beyond: A History of and Timeline of Affirmative Action" by Borgna Brunner

<http://www.infoplease.com/spot/affirmative1.html>

"The Origins of Affirmative Action" by Marquita Sykes

<http://www.now.org/nnt/08-95/affirmhs.html>

Index